Brian Dowell
Self Psychology
Kohut

What People Are Saying About *The Divine Dance...*

Humanity, says Richard Rohr, is a perfect rhyme for what Christianity, trying to express the inexpressible, calls the holy trinity. This human dance we're all in reflects a mysterious divine dance, one that we notice on our best days. Finding the sweet spot where contemporary science meets ancient mysticism, and theology meets poetry, *The Divine Dance* sketches a beautiful choreography for a life well-lived. In our joy or our pain, true life is always relational, a flow, a dance. (And was always meant to be.)

—*Bono*, U2

Seriously friends, this is Richard in peak form, doing what he does best: showing you how the best ideas for the future have actually been here, in the Jesus tradition, the whole time. In these pages it's the Trinity—that old familiar word—that suddenly gets infused with insight and electricity as you see just how practical and helpful and healing and inspiring and provocative and dangerous this conception of the Divine is. Our favorite Franciscan has done it again!

—*Rob Bell*
Speaker, teacher, and author, *Love Wins*
RobBell.com

More and more people are struggling with conventional understandings of God, like the big white guy on a throne with a long beard and a fistful of swords and lightning bolts by which you (or your enemies) might be smitten at any moment if you don't think or act correctly. For many, the concept of Trinity simply triples their God-problems. But in *The Divine Dance*, Richard Rohr and Mike Morrell explore the Trinity as a pathway beyond problematic understandings of God. This beautifully-written book can do far more than change your troubled thoughts about God: it can change your way of thinking about God entirely.

—*Brian D. McLaren*
Activist, speaker, and author, *We Make the Road by Walking*
brianmclaren.net

Rohr and Morrell have given us a liberating and yet totally orthodox invitation into the life of God. This book is a celebration of the Trinity, not as bad math (1+1+1=3), and not as baffling mystery to avoid, but as the divine movement of love. I'm grateful for a book that speaks God not with pretense and jargon, but with wisdom and genuine human experience. *The Divine Dance* is an example of why Rohr has had such a profound influence on so many Christians seeking to balance reason and mystery, action and contemplation, not to mention faith and real life.

—*Nadia Bolz-Weber*
Pastor, House for All Sinners and Saints
Author, *Accidental Saints: Finding God in All the Wrong People*
NadiaBolzWeber.com

The Divine Dance reminds us that God is a holy community—Father, Son, Spirit. And that humanity is created in the image of community, with a deep longing to love and be loved. This book calls us to be like God—to belong to each other, to be one as God is one, and to refuse to do life alone.

—*Shane Claiborne*
Activist and author, *Jesus for President*
RedLetterChristians.org

It's ironic that, while we have many religious institutions named after the Trinity, we are increasingly plagued by feelings of isolation and loneliness because we fail to truly experience this mysterious Three-In-One. With wisdom, compassion, and deep theological insight, Rohr and Morrell help readers begin to hear the music, understand the invitation, and feel the joy that leads our souls to enter into the Divine Dance.

—*Sarah Thebarge*
Author, *The Invisible Girls*
SarahThebarge.com

Richard Rohr is one of the great spiritual masters of our time, indeed of any time. His superb new book on the Trinity is vintage Rohr: clearheaded, provocative, inspiring, challenging, and, most of all, suffused with the presence of the Holy Spirit. The Trinity will of course always remain a profound mystery, but after reading Father Rohr's book, you will experience it as a mystery that can, and will, transform your life.

—*James Martin, SJ*
Author, *Jesus: A Pilgrimage* and *Seven Last Words*

The Divine Dance is a joyful plunge into what is often dry academic mystery. Richard Rohr shares his exploration into the sacred and challenges us all to come along on the nourishing journey to community.

—*Simone Campbell, SSS*
NETWORK Executive Director, lawyer, advocate, poet,
and author, *A Nun on the Bus*
NetworkLobby.org

This is Christianity, awake. In *The Divine Dance*, Fr. Rohr and Mike Morrell inspire the mind and open the heart by exploring how a more robust Trinitarian theology can enliven faith in a way that's rooted not only in Christian tradition, but in wisdom, experience, and love.

—*Michael Gungor*
Musician and author, *The Crowd, the Critic, and the Muse*
GungorMusic.com

Part devotional, part theological (re)introduction to the Holy Trinity, *The Divine Dance* sheds light on a few of the moves that will get your pew-weary muscles up and moving again. But be warned—it's hard to dance without touching!

—*Jennifer Knapp*
Singer/songwriter and author, *Facing the Music*
JenniferKnapp.com

I would never call myself a mystic, or a contemplative. My life of faith runs at warp speed. The Creator inspires me to produce worship that is cacophonous and joyful; Jesus catapults me into battles for a more just society; and the Spirit tosses me into rigorous loving of neighbor and self. This lovely book caused me to slow down, to be present, to attend and be curious about the partners in the Divine Dance. I felt as though Father Rohr was sitting with me at tea, that Mike Morrell was with us, weaving language, painting an intimate portrait of God, Jesus, and Holy Spirit—the mystery of the Trinity. Each Person is more alive, now, circling in my heart—is it a waltz? A two-step? Even hip-hop? This book must be on your shelf: clergy, lay leaders, activists, and academics. For reflection and sustenance. To remember our "likeness" with Holy. To be invited to the dance.

—*The Rev. Dr. Jacqui Lewis*
Senior Minister, Middle Collegiate Church (New York City)
Host, Just Faith (MSNBC.com); author, *The Power of Stories*
JacquiJLewis.com

The three are one? Well, yes. One dynamic reality, one joyful noise, one glorious flowing explosion of sacred suchness! A daring doctrine indeed. As a Jewish Hindu Buddhist Sufi, I finally get it. God is love and love is unendingly unfolding—permeating and transforming and connecting All That Is. *The Divine Dance* may well be Richard Rohr's most important book.

—*Mirabai Starr*
Author, *God of Love: A Guide to the Heart of Judaism, Christianity and Islam*
MirabaiStarr.com

The Divine Dance is not only Richard Rohr's best book; it's the best book on the Trinity I've ever read. Tender, human, both pastorally and psychologically brilliant, this is the work Rohr was born to do—the theological master grid that illumines a lifetime of teaching. While the depth and the scope of the book are enormous, *The Divine Dance* is most marked by its shimmering, revelatory clarity. The writing, like our three-in-one God, dances. For Rohr and Morrell, the Trinity is not just the revelation of God but the revelation of everything. I wept, I worshipped, I started all over again. An instant spiritual classic.

—*Jonathan Martin*
Author, *How to Survive a Shipwreck*
JonathanMartinWords.com

This book is essential to anyone who has ever suffered under the impression of an angry King God who sits on a throne and judges the wicked. *The Divine Dance* illuminates the beautiful implications of a God who is truly Father, Son, and Holy Spirit, whose very being is formed by relationship—and in doing so reclaims the essential good of Christian belief.

—*Mike McHargue*
Author, *Finding God in the Waves*
MikeMcHargue.com

The Divine Dance is a radical rediscovery of the Trinity for our generation, providing an expanded understanding of the divine flow of the Trinity and how it provides a framework for everything…our relationships, our sexuality, our self-worth, and our spirituality. It's an enlightening read for all Christians who have struggled to understand the Trinity beyond an impersonal doctrine, and illuminates how the integration of the Trinity sets us all on a path to spiritual integration, vulnerability, and wholeness.

—*Kristen Howerton*
Writer
rageagainsttheminivan.com

The Divine Dance invites you into the heart of Christian mysticism: the lavish ever-expanding love of God. Richard Rohr and Mike Morrell show how the triune God is more than a philosophical concept—the Trinity is a joyous celebration of love and life, and we are all called to participate. This is not a book merely to be read or studied; it is meant to be *lived*.

—*Carl McColman*
Author, *The Big Book of Christian Mysticism*
CarlMcColman.net

One of the most misunderstood and underappreciated doctrines in the modern church is beginning to see a resurgence as humanity moves into a non-dualistic age of consciousness that is discovering the beauty and power of the mystery of our three-in-one, relational God. In *The Divine Dance*, Fr. Richard Rohr and Mike Morrell explore the depths of the Trinitarian mystery in a surprisingly accessible and refreshing manner, reflecting on how Christianity's triune conception of God holds the keys to personal and societal transformation.

This book is a truly vital re-presentation of the fundamental truths that lie at the heart of the Christian gospel for a new age. Rohr and Morrell have written a soon-to-be classic that will re-enchant many with the beauty of the Christian tradition while causing us to expand and explore beyond the boundaries of rigid religiosity. This book is practical, profound, and inspiring, a must-read for every Christian in the twenty-first century.

—*Brandan Robertson*
Author, *Nomad: A Spirituality for Travelling Light*
BrandanRobertson.com

With the wisdom of C.S. Lewis and the accessibility of Rob Bell, Richard Rohr and Mike Morrell unpack our long-lingering questions about God, love, grace, and forgiveness, all through the lens of Trinitarian spirituality. This isn't to say that this book answers every question. Like all good mystics, Rohr and Morrell circle our questions, reveling in the mystery of all that is. Join them. Stand with them "under the waterfall of God's infinite mercy, and know that you are loved."

—*David James Poissant*
L.A. Times Book Prize Finalist; author, *The Heaven of Animals*
davidjamespoissant.com

Many years ago I had a vision—somehow I just knew—of the Trinity, dancing. In this dance God's persons were filled with great contagious joy. I remember wishing I could join them in that intimate, circular dance. You can imagine my great joy when Jesus took me by the hand and included me in it!

My dear friend Richard Rohr has once again given us a remarkable book on a subject that most Christians haven't really thought about or prayed about, and yet we all agree is at the very heart of Christianity: this very Trinity. Richard's heart is to reform Christianity from the bottom up by making clear the very shape of God, and in *The Divine Dance* he does just that. I am very privileged to endorse this marvelous book and to know that the wisdom contained within these pages will enable us all to join in the dance of life!

—*Francis MacNutt*
Healing minister and author, *The Healing Reawakening*
christianhealingmin.org

Though my heritage is in the charismatic movement, I've always had a spiritual curiosity that led me beyond the borders of my traditional upbringing. I believe that there is a faith available that far exceeds any fear of being deceived. If we are honest, all of us have questioned what we believed in the past in order to arrive at the beliefs we have in the present. *The Divine Dance* is the perfect catalyst for continued trailblazing.

I have a love affair with progressive thinkers like Richard Rohr and Mike Morrell who courageously challenge truths that have become static and have lost their relevance. Their generational collaboration with this work is critical for those of us evolving in our theological perspectives. Together, they demonstrate an intelligent humility, teaching the reader how to think instead of what to think.

Within these pages, I discovered that what I have known about the Trinity was not necessarily inaccurate, just incomplete. *Dance* is a perfect metaphor for engaging with mystery. Rohr and Morrell accepted the invitation of the Father, Son, and Spirit—an invitation that asks, "May I have this dance?" From the first chapter, I was taken by the hand and swept off my feet, gliding, dipping, and pirouetting into the deep insights of the Trinity. My heart is still dancing. This is, hands down, the very best theological treatise I have read in forty years.

—*Dr. Randall Worley*
Author, *Brush Strokes of Grace*
RandallWorley.com

I didn't think I needed to understand the hypostatic unity of the Trinity; I just needed to turn my life over to whoever made the Grand Canyon. Reading *The Divine Dance* gives me the same feeling—I want to get up and move!

—*Kevin Prosch*
Singer, songwriter, and recording artist

Richard Rohr has done it again! In *The Divine Dance*, Richard and Mike Morrell reveal the spiritual paradigm shift that is taking place for us to reexamine how we see God. God is not some far-away threatener but the life-source in all things! This book is life-changing and will make you take a second look at who God really is within creation. Well done! *The Divine Dance* is top-notch and a must-read!

—*Jeremy Lopez*
Author, *The Power of the Eternal Now*
Founder, Identitynetwork.net

The Divine Dance is a love story, calling us forward to embrace the fullness of God in the unitive three parts of God's self. Fr. Richard Rohr and Mike Morrell invite us to unleash our limited God images—often made small by our vision of singular or separated Father, Son, and Holy Spirit.

These pages call us to consciously reunite our God of three to see the full expression of God's being—like a waterwheel, God flows freely as parts flowing into wholeness.

The Divine Dance offers us the opportunity to fall in love with a robust God, and in doing so, gives us the gift of a divine mirror, which sees and loves us completely, and allows us to embrace and fully love ourselves.

—*Teresa B. Mateus, LCSW*
Author, *Sacred Wounds: A Path to Healing from Spiritual Trauma*
teresabmateus.com

Richard Rohr is a friend and contemplative and has taught us so much about the joys of a deep inner spiritual life. In *The Divine Dance: The Trinity and Your Transformation*, Richard maturely explains the nature and deep meaning of the Trinity, which has gone unappreciated by many Christians for much of the last seventeen hundred years. I strongly recommend this book to anyone who wants to understand the relationship between human beings and God more richly and deeply.

—*Jim Wallis*
President of Sojourners and editor-in-chief of *Sojourners* magazine
New York Times best-selling author, *America's Original Sin*

THE DIVINE DANCE

THE TRINITY AND YOUR TRANSFORMATION

THE DIVINE DANCE

THE TRINITY AND YOUR TRANSFORMATION

RICHARD ROHR

WITH MIKE MORRELL

WHITAKER
HOUSE

Photo of Mike Morrell by Marc LeMauviel, www.litewerk.com.

The Divine Dance:
The Trinity and Your Transformation
Hardcover Edition

Richard Rohr
cac.org

ISBN: 978-1-62911-729-4
eBook ISBN: 978-1-62911-730-0
Printed in the United States of America
© 2016 by Richard Rohr

Whitaker House
1030 Hunt Valley Circle
New Kensington, PA 15068
www.whitakerhouse.com

LC record available at https://lccn.loc.gov/2016037109.

3 4 5 6 7 8 9 10 11 12 **W** 23 22 21 20 19 18 17 16

CONTENTS

PART I
WANTED: A TRINITARIAN REVOLUTION

PART II
WHY THE TRINITY? WHY NOW?

PART III
THE HOLY SPIRIT

DEDICATION

FROM RICHARD ROHR

To all the unsuspecting folks who do not know they are already within the Divine Flow.

FROM MIKE MORRELL

To my daughters, Jubilee Grace and Nova Rain. You embody Spirit's unexpected movements in my life!

FOREWORD

ONE alone
    is not by nature Love,
            or Laugh,
            or Sing
ONE alone
    may be Prime Mover,
            Unknowable
            Indivisible
            All
    and if Everything is All and All is One
            One is Alone
            Self-Centered
                Not Love
                Not Laugh
                Not Sing

TWO
    Ying/Yang
    Dark/Light
    Male/Female
        contending Dualism
            Affirming Evil/Good
            And striving toward Balance
        At best Face-to-Face
            but Never Community
THREE
    Face-to-Face-to-Face
        Community
        Ambiguity
        Mystery
    Love for the Other
        And for the Other's Love
    Within
        Other-Centered
        Self-Giving
            Loving
            Singing
            Laughter
                A fourth is created
                Ever-loved and loving.

Relationship has always been the wild card, the court jester who appears in the midst of our human agenda and our hallucinations of independent self-sufficiency, revealing by any means that the emperor is naked.

When you even skim the edges of relationship, you submit to mystery and lose control. Marriage would be so much easier if there wasn't another person involved, but then it would be meaningless, too. Relationships are entwined, entrenched, elusive, messy, enabling, enrapturing, maddening, exhilarating, frustrating, exposing, and too beautiful for words. There are moments when we think we might finally have a whisper of control over our world, and then—*whoosh!*—in comes someone who knocks it completely sideways.

Yet it is relationship that provides the backdrop and framing for the art of our lives, apart from which our colors would simply disperse into the darkness formless and void, awaiting the hovering of the Spirit to collect them and—with Her shades and hues—breathe into us to set them free.

Bad theology is like pornography—the imagination of a real relationship without the risk of one. It tends to be transactional and propositional rather than relational and mysterious. You don't have to trust Person, or care for Person. It becomes an exercise in self-gratification that ultimately dehumanizes the self and the community of humanity in order to avoid the painful processes of humbling and trusting. Bad theology is not a victimless crime. It dehumanizes God and turns the wonder and the messy mystery of intimate relationship into a centerfold to be used and discarded.

There is a rising rumble, like a midnight train approaching through the wastelands. Not only do we hear it from the distance, but we can feel it if we put our hands on the ground or in the water or in the torn bread and poured-out wine. The rumor in the deep places of our souls is that there is a party going on, and we can scarce trust our invitation. Could there ever be a toast raised to us? Might a hand reach out and lead us into the *divine dance*, whispering in our ears that we were always made for this? And so we wait for the kiss, the breath in and out that awakens our sleeping hearts to life. We were made for this, utterly found within Relentless Affection!

There is a community of intelligent mystics who are speaking with profound compassion and authenticity, daring to accept this table fellowship themselves, and reminding us that *we, too*, received an invitation. Richard

Rohr and Mike Morrell are two of these voices, calling us forward and inviting us to actively change what we let into our hearts, calling us to consciously participate in this divine dance of loving and being loved.

We have watched the waters recede over the last few hundred years, and with this came a sense of ebbing hope. But as we challenge and change what we let into our hearts, we realize this: we have *not* been forsaken or abandoned, and what we thought we were losing was really a gathering. Waters made of many voices rise into a fountain of life that is collecting dreams—of expectancy and chronic wonder and longing love—the cusp of a new reformation and the release of renaissance. As wonderful as revival has been, it has never been enough. We have witnessed the shattering of the old wineskins and watched the bloodred wine be absorbed into the ground. For those with eyes to see, they look out from a towering, rising mass of living water that is about to crash upon this planet. For those whose eyes have not yet been healed—those "born blind"—although we cannot see it, we can feel it coming.

The children of this approaching re-formation of the very ways we think and see will respond quickly and easily. The elders of the empires will take much more work. They are not to be discarded, though, for love never rejects a single bit of bread or drop of wine.

The Divine Dance, along with thousands of other rising voices, is a violation of Empire and a celebration of Relationship. When one has seen the profound mysteries lovingly revealed here, one cannot un-see. When one has heard, there is no going back; suffering cannot wipe away the heart's smile.

God, You have never had a low view of Humanity.

May our eyes be healed, especially those of us "born blind," that we might see what You do.

May our ears be opened to the music that heals, celebrating the entanglement of differences so that even in our discord, we hear that we ourselves are the melody embraced in Three-Part Harmony.

May our courage be emboldened to take the risks of trust, to live only inside the grace of one single day, to reach across Empire's borders and tear down the walls that mask our faces.

May we feel within us the eternal life of Jesus reaching through our hands—to heal, to hold, to hug—and celebrate the bread of our Humanity, the sanctity of the Ordinary and Participation in the Trinity.

As you read these pages and live your lives, may it be so!

—William Paul Young
Author, *The Shack, Cross Roads,* and *Eve*
Trinity Sunday, 2016

INTRODUCTION:
"SIX IMPOSSIBLE THINGS BEFORE BREAKFAST"

The Blessed Trinity is supposed to be a central—even the paramount—foundational doctrine of our entire Christian belief system. And yet we're told, at least I was told as a young boy in Kansas, that we shouldn't try to understand it.

"Just believe it!" we were admonished. But there it stopped. Irish-born Sister Ephrem just held up the shamrock to my totally trustful third-grade class. We surely believed, if not in the Trinity, at least in her earnest Irish faith. (Although maybe that is exactly how the divine flow has to start! *With sharing a bit of earnest and deep goodness.*)

Yet it was indeed a mystery. Sort of a mathematical conundrum to test our ability to believe impossible things to be true. You would have thought "believing six impossible things before breakfast" was the actual goal of my pre-Vatican II Catholic training. But later, I found my Protestant friends had approximately the same approach to faith; it merely involved different impossibilities, usually things that happened in the Bible. They didn't seem to appreciate inner experience too much, either.

And here I am, some sixty years later, presuming to try to breach this impenetrable mystery. Shall we dare to try?

I suppose this is the only real way we can join in the dance…

TRINITY: MIA

Let's begin with the shocking and oft-quoted idea from Karl Rahner, the German Jesuit who was such a major influence at the Second Vatican Council. In his classic study *The Trinity*, he said, "Christians are, in their practical life, almost mere 'monotheists.' We must be willing to admit that, should the doctrine of the Trinity have to be dropped as false, the major part of religious literature could well remain virtually unchanged."[1]

We would have to admit this was largely true until William Paul Young wrote his worldwide best-selling novel, *The Shack*, in the past decade.[2] For the first time since fourth-century Cappadocia, the Trinity actually became an inspired subject of conversation and rather pleasant questioning in homes and restaurants. And it continues!

But seventeen centuries of being missing in action—how could this have been true? Could this absence help us understand how we might still be in the infancy stage of Christianity? Could it help explain the simple ineffectiveness and lack of transformation we witness in so much of the Christian world? When you are off at the center, the whole edifice is quite shaky and unsure of itself.

If Trinity is supposed to describe the very heart of the nature of God, and yet it has almost no practical or pastoral implications in most of our lives…if it's even possible that we could drop it tomorrow and it would be a forgettable, throwaway doctrine…*then either it can't be true or we don't understand it!*

Since you're reading this, I'm going to guess that, somewhere, you believe it must somehow be true. In the pages that follow, I'm going to simply circle around this most paradoxical idea about the nature of God. And in truth, *circling around* is actually an apt metaphor for this mystery that we're trying to apprehend. There is no other way to appreciate mystery.

1. Karl Rahner, *The Trinity* (New York: Crossroad Publishing Company, 1999), 10–11.
2. William Paul Young, *The Shack* (Newbury Park, CA: Windblown Media, 2007).

Remember, mystery isn't something that you *cannot* understand—it is something that you can *endlessly understand*! There is no point at which you can say, "I've got it." Always and forever, mystery gets *you*!

"Circling around" is all we can do. Our speaking of God is a search for similes, analogies, and metaphors. All theological language is an approximation, offered tentatively in holy awe. That's the best human language can achieve. We can say, *"It's like—it's similar to…,"* but we can never say, *"It is…"* because we are in the realm of beyond, of transcendence, of mystery. And we must—absolutely must—maintain a fundamental humility before the Great Mystery. If we do not, religion always worships itself and its formulations and never God.

The very mystical Cappadocian Fathers of fourth-century eastern Turkey eventually developed some highly sophisticated thinking on what we soon called the Trinity. It took three centuries of reflection on the Gospels to have the courage to say it, but they of this land—which included Paul of Tarsus before them and Mevlânâ Rumi of Konya afterward—*circled around* to the best metaphor they could find:

Whatever is going on in God is a *flow*, a *radical relatedness*, a *perfect communion* between Three—a circle dance of love.

And God is not just a dancer; God is the dance itself. Now hold on to this. This is not some new, trendy theology from America. This is about as traditional as you can get. Here it is in the words of Brother Elias Marechal, a monk at the Monastery of the Holy Spirit in Conyers, Georgia:

The ancient Greek Fathers depict the Trinity as a Round Dance: an event that has continued for six thousand years, and six times six thousand, and beyond the time when humans *first* knew time. An infinite current of love streams without ceasing, *to and fro, to and fro, to and fro*: gliding from the Father to the Son, and back to the Father, in one timeless happening. This circular current of trinitarian love continues night and day…. The orderly and rhythmic process of subatomic particles spinning round and round at immense speed echoes its dynamism.[3]

---

3. Elias Marechal, *Tears of an Innocent God* (New York: Paulist Press, 2015), 7.

Here it is: the "circle dance" of the Trinity is *very* traditional language. And yet if I showed the same courage to use such a risky theatrical word today, I would probably be called New Age, an esoteric—or a heretic.

Yet God is the dance itself, they said!

A SPACE AT GOD'S TABLE

Let's observe this *divine dance* in an enigmatic story from the very first book of our sacred texts that we call the Bible.

> The Lord appeared to Abraham near the great trees of Mamre while he was sitting at the entrance to his tent in the heat of the day. Abraham looked up and saw three men standing nearby. When he saw them, he hurried from the entrance of his tent to meet them and bowed low to the ground.
>
> He said, "If I have found favor in your eyes, my lord, do not pass your servant by. Let a little water be brought, and then you may all wash your feet and rest under this tree. Let me get you something to eat, so you can be refreshed and then go on your way—now that you have come to your servant."
>
> "Very well," they answered, "do as you say."
>
> So Abraham hurried into the tent to Sarah. "Quick," he said, "get three seahs of the finest flour and knead it and bake some bread."
>
> Then he ran to the herd and selected a choice, tender calf and gave it to a servant, who hurried to prepare it. He then brought some curds and milk and the calf that had been prepared, and set these before them. While they ate, he stood near them under a tree.[4]

This account gives us a lot to chew on. The scene is set up as "*the* Lord" appearing to Abraham, but in the realm of discernable form, those appearing to him are seen as "*three men.*"

In the centuries of reflection, theology, and storytelling that have followed this original story, these three are often regarded as angels, and perhaps something more. Abraham—bowing low before them—seems to

---

4. Genesis 18:1–8 (NIV).

intuitively recognize this *something more* and invites them to a meal and a rest. He does not join them in the meal but observes them eating from afar, standing *"under a tree."* A place at God's table is still too much to imagine.

Abraham and Sarah seem to see the Holy One in the presence of the three, and their first instinct is one of invitation and hospitality—to create a space of food and drink for them. Here we have humanity still feeding God; it will take a long time to turn that around in the human imagination. "Surely, we ourselves are not invited to this divine table," they presume.

This unique and multifaceted story inspired an equally unique and multifaceted piece of devotional religious art entitled *The Hospitality of Abraham*—also called, simply (and for reasons we'll get into) *The Trinity*.

I believe all genuine art is sacred. Self-consciously "religious" art is often trying too hard and descends into cheap sentiment. But the particular form of artistic expression *The Trinity* belongs to—the icon—attempts to point beyond itself, inviting in its viewers a sense of both the *beyond* and the *communion* that exists in our midst.

Created by Russian iconographer Andrei Rublev in the fifteenth century, *The Trinity* is the icon of icons for many of us—and, as I would discover years after first encountering it, even more invitational than most. By my lights, it is the most perfect piece of religious art there is; I've always had a copy of it hanging in my room. The original is still on display in the Tretyakov gallery in Moscow.

There's a story told that one artist became a follower of Jesus just from gazing at this icon, exclaiming, "If that's the nature of God, then I'm a believer." And I can fully understand this.

In Rublev's icon there are three primary colors, which illustrate facets of the Holy One, all contained in the Three.

Rublev considered *gold* the color of "the Father"—perfection, fullness, wholeness, the ultimate Source.

He considered *blue* the color of "the Human"—both sea and sky mirroring one another—and therefore God in Christ taking on the world, taking on humanity. Thus, Rublev pictures the Christ as blue, displaying his two fingers to tell us that he has put spirit and matter, divinity and humanity, together within himself—and for us!

And then there's *green*, easily representative of "the Spirit." Hildegard of Bingen, the German Benedictine abbess, musical composer, writer, philosopher, mystic, and overall visionary, living three centuries before Rublev, called the Spirit's endless fertility and fecundity *veriditas*—a quality of divine aliveness that makes everything blossom and bloom in endless shades of green.

Hildegard was likely inspired by the lushness of her surroundings at her Rhineland monastery, which I was recently able to visit. Rublev, in similar reverence for the natural world, chose green to represent, as it were, the *divine photosynthesis* that grows everything from within by *transforming light into itself*—precisely the work of the Holy Spirit.

Is that good or what?

The Holy One in the form of Three—eating and drinking, in infinite hospitality and utter enjoyment between themselves. If we take the depiction of God in *The Trinity* seriously, we have to say, "In the beginning was the Relationship."

This icon yields more fruits the more you gaze on it. Every part of it was obviously meditated on with great care: the gaze between the Three; the deep respect between them as they all share from a common bowl. And note the hand of the Spirit pointing toward the open and fourth place at the table! Is the Holy Spirit inviting, offering, and clearing space? If so, for what?

A (W)HOLE IN GOD

As magnificent as this icon—and this fellowship—is…there's something missing.

They're circling a shared table, and if you look on the front of the table there appears to be a little rectangular *hole* painted there. Most people just pass right over it, but art historians say that the remaining glue on the original icon indicates that there was perhaps once a *mirror* glued to the front of the table!

If you don't come from an Orthodox, Catholic, or Anglican background, this might not strike you as odd, but you should know that this is a most unusual feature for an icon. One would normally not put a real mirror on the front of a holy icon. If so, it is entirely unique and courageous.

This might have been Rublev's final design flourish. Or maybe it was added later—we're not sure.

But can you imagine what its meaning might be?

It's stunning when you think about it—there was room at this table for a *fourth*.

The observer.

You!

At the heart of Christian revelation, God is not seen as a distant, static monarch but—as we will explore together—a *divine circle dance*, as the early Fathers of the church dared to call it (in Greek *perichoresis*, the origin of our word *choreography*). God is the Holy One presenced in the dynamic and loving action of Three.

But even this Three-Fullness does not like to eat alone. This invitation to share at the divine table is probably the first biblical hint of what we would eventually call "salvation."

Jesus comes forth from this Eternal Fullness, allowing us to see ourselves mirrored, as a part of this table fellowship—as a participant at this banquet and as a partner in God's eternal dance of love and communion.

The mirror seems to have been lost over the centuries, both in the icon and in our on-the-ground understanding of who God is and who we therefore are, created in God's "image and likeness."[5]

My fondest hope would be that these pages would reposition you in the mirror of divine fellowship, with a place at the table.

I want you to take this image into yourself as you read. I invite you to recognize that this Table is not reserved exclusively for the Three, nor is the divine circle dance a closed circle: we're all invited in. All creation is invited in, and this is the liberation God intended from the very beginning.

---

5. See Genesis 1:26–27.

This divine intention—this audacious invitation—is embedded in creation itself;[6] it later becomes concrete, personal, and touchable in Jesus.[7] In other words, divine inclusion—again, what we rightly name *salvation*—was Plan A and not Plan B!

Our final goal of union with God is grounded in creation itself, and also in our own unique creation.[8] This was a central belief in my own spiritual formation as a Franciscan friar.[9] Our starting place was always *original goodness*,[10] not original sin. This makes our ending place—and everything in between—possessing an inherent capacity for goodness, truth, and beauty.

Salvation is not some occasional, later emergency additive but God's ultimate intention from the very beginning, even "written in our hearts."[11]

Are you ready to take your place at this wondrous table? Can you imagine that you are already a part of the dance?

Then let's begin to explore both how and why!

---

6. See John 1:1–18; Colossians 1:15–20; Ephesians 1:3–14; Romans 1:20; 8:18–25.
7. See, for example, 1 John 1:1–3; Hebrews 1:1–3.
8. See, for example, Ephesians 1:3–4.
9. See Richard Rohr, *Eager to Love* (Cincinnati, OH: Franciscan Media, 2014), app. I, 209, which explores how *Christ* and *Jesus* are two different but overlapping truths.
10. See Genesis 1:10–31.
11. See Jeremiah 31:33; Hebrews 8:10; 10:16.

PART I
WANTED: A TRINITARIAN REVOLUTION

SPIRITUAL PARADIGM SHIFT

God did not send His Son into the world to condemn the world, but that the world through Him might be saved.[12]

My Father goes on working, and so do I.[13]

The Holy Spirit...will teach you all things and will remind you of everything I have said to you.[14]

Before you try to figure out why I started this section with these three separate citations about a very active and involved God, let me try to explain. And all I can ever do is *try*.

In his book *The Structure of Scientific Revolutions*, Thomas Kuhn popularized the word "paradigm shift."[15] He made clear that even in the scientific field, a paradigm shift is tantamount to what religion often calls "major conversion." And it is equally rare in both science and religion! Any genuine transformation of worldview asks for such a major switch from the track we're familiar with that often those who hold the old paradigm must actually die off before a new paradigm can gain traction and wide acceptance. Even more shocking is Kuhn's conclusion that a paradigm shift has little to do with logic or even evidence, and everything to do with cataclysmic insight and breakthrough. German mystic Meister Eckhart called this phenomenon "boiling."[16]

At the risk of sounding like I am making a serious overstatement, I think the common Christian image of God, despite Jesus, is still largely "pagan" (not that pagans are bad people, by the way!) and untransformed.

What do I mean by this? History has so long operated with *a static and imperial image of God*—as a Supreme Monarch who is mostly living in splendid isolation from what he—and God is always and exclusively

---

12. John 3:17 (NKJV).
13. John 5:17 (JB).
14. John 14:26 (NIV).
15. See *The Structure of Scientific Revolutions*, 4th ed. (Chicago: University of Chicago Press, 2012).
16. See, for example, *Meister Eckhart: The Essential Sermons, Commentaries, Treatises and Defense* (Classics of Western Spirituality), rev. ed. (New York: Paulist Press, 1981), 37.

envisioned as male in this model—created. This God is seen largely as a Critical Spectator (and his followers do their level best to imitate their Creator in this regard).

We always become what we behold; the presence that we practice matters. That's why we desperately need a worldwide paradigm shift in Christian consciousness regarding how we relate to God. This shift has been subtly yet profoundly underway for some time, hiding in plain sight—the revelation of God as what we have always called "Trinity" but have barely understood (*in the beginning was the Relationship*).

This slowly-dawning Christian revelation was supposed to have radically changed our image of God, but for the most part it did not. The old wiring was just too much in place. It has taken us two thousand years to try to make this shift; but now history, mental health, so many negative and angry Christians, cosmology, and quantum physics are quickly demanding it of us.

Kuhn said that paradigm shifts become necessary when the plausibility structure of the previous paradigm becomes so full of holes and patchwork "fixes" that a complete overhaul, which once looked utterly threatening, now appears as a lifeline.

I believe we're at precisely such a moment when it comes to our images of God. Instead of the idea of Trinity being an abstruse conundrum, it could well end up being the answer to the foundational problem of Western religion.

Instead of God being the Eternal Threatener, we have God as the Ultimate Participant—in everything—both the good and the painful.

Let me try to describe the two paradigms in stark contrast.

Instead of an Omnipotent Monarch, let's try what God as Trinity demonstrates as the actual and wondrous shape of the Divine Reality, which then *replicates itself in us*[17] and in "all the array" of creation.[18]

Instead of God watching life happen from afar and judging it…

How about God being inherent in *life itself?*

17. See Genesis 1:26.
18. See Genesis 2:1.

How about God being *the Life Force of everything?*

Instead of God being an Object like any other object...

How about God being *the Life Energy between each and every object* (which we would usually call *Love* or *Spirit*)?

This allows God to be much larger, *at least* coterminous with the ever-larger universe we are discovering, and *totally inclusive*—what else could any God worthy of the name be?

Instead of the small god we seem stuck with in our current (and dying) paradigm, usually preoccupied with exclusion, the Trinitarian Revolution reveals God as *with us in all of life* instead of standing on the sidelines, always critiquing which things belong and which things don't.

The Trinitarian Revolution reveals God as *always involved* instead of the in-and-out deity that leaves most of humanity "orphaned" much of the time.[19]

Theologically, of course, this revolution repositions grace as inherent to creation, not as an occasional additive that some people occasionally merit.

If this revolution has always been quietly present, like yeast in the dough of our rising spirituality, it might help us understand the hopeful and positive "adoption" and "inheritance" theologies of Paul[20] and the Eastern Fathers over the later, punitive images of God that have dominated the Western church.

This God is the very one whom we have named "Trinity"—the *flow* who flows through everything, without exception, and who has done so since the beginning.

Thus, everything is holy, for those who have learned how to see.

The implications of this spiritual paradigm shift, this Trinitarian Revolution, are staggering: every vital impulse, every force toward the future, every creative momentum, every loving surge, every dash toward beauty, every running toward truth, every ecstasy before simple goodness, every leap of *élan vital,* as the French would say, every bit of ambition

---

19. See John 14:18.
20. See, for example, Romans 8:14–17; Galatians 4:5–7; Ephesians 1:5, 14.

for humanity and the earth, for wholeness and holiness, is the eternally-flowing life of the Trinitarian God.

Whether we know it or not! *This is not an invitation that you can agree with or disagree with. It is a description of what is already happening in God and in everything created in God's image and likeness.*

This triune God allows you, impels you, to live easily with God everywhere and all the time: in the budding of a plant, the smile of a gardener, the excitement of a teenage boy over his new girlfriend, the tireless determination of a research scientist, the pride of a mechanic over his hidden work under the hood, the loving nuzzling of horses, the tenderness with which eagles feed their chicks, and the downward flow of every mountain stream.

This God is found even in the suffering and death of those very things! How could this not be the life-energy of God? How could it be anything else? Such a big definition of life must include death in its Great Embrace, "so that none of your labors will be wasted."[21]

In the chirp of every bird excited about a new morning, in the hard beauty of every sandstone cliff, in the deep satisfaction at every job well done, in the passion of sex, and even in a clerk's gratuitous smile to a department store customer or in the passivity of the hospital bed, *"the world, life or death, the present or the future—all belong to you; [and] you belong to Christ and Christ belongs to God,"* as the apostle Paul puts it.[22] It is one Trinitarian Flow since the beginning.

Unless God's seers can begin to make this paradigm shift, there is no way that God is going to be able to "save the world." Courtroom scenes and penal systems do not inspire or change the world. They are totally inadequate to communicate the Divine Banquet and invitation; in fact, they make it largely impossible to imagine. It is not about being obviously religious. We have tried that for centuries with small results; it's about being quietly joyous and cooperative[23] with the divine *generosity* that connects everything to everything else.

---

21. See 1 Corinthians 15:51–58.
22. 1 Corinthians 3:22–23.
23. See Romans 8:28.

Yes, *God* is saving the world, and God goes on working even though we fail to notice, fail to enjoy, fail to pass on, and fail to fully live our one and only life. We become like the small god we have too often worshipped, and thus spectators at our own funeral.

How about this, instead:

There is only Christ: he is everything and he is in everything.[24]

When Christ is [fully] revealed—and he is your life—you too will be revealed in all your glory with him.[25]

A revolution is already underway; the old plausibility structures of divinity are diminishing; so much of religion is in rigor mortis. Are we ready to let go of what's no longer working and embrace the paradigm that has always been emerging and is always too much for us? As St. Augustine said, this God is "ever ancient and ever new."

If my instincts are right, this unearthing of Trinity can't come a moment too soon. Because I'm convinced that beneath the ugly manifestations of our present evils—political corruption, ecological devastation, warring against one another, hating each other based on race, gender, religion, or sexual orientation—the greatest dis-ease facing humanity right now is our profound and painful sense of *disconnection*.

Disconnection from God, certainly, but also from ourselves (our bodies), from each other, and from our world.

Our sense of this fourfold isolation is plunging us as a culture—as a species—into increasingly destructive behavior. While our world is not as doom and gloom as those who feed on a steady diet of cable TV and social media-driven "bad news" might conclude, it's true that the sheer scope and complexity of our disconnection is staggering.

I'm discovering that the gift of the Trinity—and our practical, felt experience of receiving this gift—offers a grounded reconnection with God, self, others, and world that all religion and spirituality, and arguably,

---

24. Colossians 3:11.
25. Colossians 3:4 (JB).

even politics, is aiming for—but which conventional religion, spirituality, and politics fall short of.

The religion, spirituality, and politics of worthiness games, belonging barriers, and achievement rewards will never be the cure: these are in fact part of the dis-ease. But God's joyous unveiling as Trinity can melt even the most hardened constrictions, illuminating the way toward a fourfold *re-union* of Spirit, self, society, and sense of space.

Are you ready to explore how a shift in our perspective from God as "removed one" to God as "most moved Mover,"[26] intimately participating in ongoing co-creation, makes such a joyous re-union possible?

If so, welcome to *The Divine Dance*. In these pages, we will indeed get to know the Trinity and the transformation of all things—including yourself.

DUSTING OFF A DARING DOCTRINE

Let me tell you a bit about how I came to more consciously participate in the divine dance. Some years ago, I had a wonderful extended time in a hermitage in Arizona during Lent. My main practices while there were to pay attention, listen, and keep a journal. Toward the end of my time there, I decided the appropriate thing to do would be to read through the journal that I'd kept to see if God had taught me anything; I wanted to see if there was any pattern to the unfolding of those wonderful and lonely days.

I went up to the Center Library, some distance from the hermitage, and there on a table was the late Catherine Mowry LaCugna's heady book entitled *God for Us: The Trinity and Christian Life*.[27] It's a big book filled with footnotes, and it looked formidable. Even so, I felt a great urging toward it, even though I hadn't intended to read anything except the Bible during this sojourn.

So instead of reading my journal in those final hermitage days, I began to slowly read this highly academic book. As I read, while catching only glimpses of understanding, I still kept saying, "*Yes, yes!*" to new words and only slightly-captured ideas. I felt the presence of a Big Tradition, which

---

26. See Clark Pinnock, *Most Moved Mover: A Theology of God's Openness* (Grand Rapids, MI: Baker Academic, 2001).
27. Harper San Francisco, 1991.

the author was tracing, naming the same inner dynamism that had been growing in me for thirty-some days. It was no longer an abstract idea, a doctrine, or a shelved "belief" but almost a phenomenology of my own— and others'—inner experience of God.

Trinity was not a belief but a very objective way of describing my own deep inner experience of Transcendence—and what I call here *flow!* Yet the conviction came from within now, and it was nothing like conforming to anything imposed from the outside. Was I kidding myself? How could such seeming objectivity and such personal subjectivity coincide so well within me?

This is it, I felt. *This sums up what I think I've experienced during this hermitage time, and maybe throughout my life.* Something was resonating, even through this heavy and often boring book (which I wouldn't even recommend unless you have some background in theology). Yet I could not put it down until I finished it the very last day of my alone time.

I had broken my intention not to read, and yet this did not feel like reading at all but being let in on a secret—a secret that I myself was.

I drove out of Arizona with a grateful inner smile, taking full, fresh breaths of the clean desert air. I much more consciously enjoyed the flow that I now saw flowing everywhere.

I'm sure this is the ultimate presumption: to think that I could understand or have anything to say about this life in the Trinity. And yet, I also feel we must use the language and experience that is available to us rather than remain silent.

I would ask you, if possible, to sink into this. Maybe this book will be more of a meditation than a scholarly treatise.

But from a deeper place, if you can allow it, my prayer and desire is that something you encounter in these pages will resonate with your own experience, so you can say, *I know this—I've witnessed this to be true for myself.*

Because *that's* the great moment in all divine revelation, when beautiful ideas drop in from head to heart, from the level of dogma to experience. When it's not something that we merely believe, but in a real sense something that we *know*.

This is my prayer: that the *divine dance* of God be something you know, and my words will not get in the way of it.

MATH PROBLEMS

Once taken for granted in Western civilization, "God" is now one of the most contested ideas we have. Debates have been argued and wars have been waged and hearts have been broken over trying to own, define, or even relate to this being—or get over its (non)existence.

Perhaps the way out of this cultural impasse is *in*:

What's going on inside of God?

How does this life express itself—manifest itself—in the dance of creation?

Followers of Jesus have long wrestled with this question in the context of God as a unity in diversity.

A Trinity...

But God is one![28]

This is the great affirmation of the three great monotheistic religions—Judaism, Christianity, and Islam. But after Jesus, most Christians defect for all practical purposes, saying, "Well, God is most perfectly revealed as Three, but he is still really One!" No wonder our Jewish ancestors were confused and said it sounded like gobbledygook to them, and a major threat to monotheism—and it came from one of their very own! Maybe this was just a mathematical conundrum? Or simply pure heresy from some esoteric group?

Not exactly One, Christian mystics and teachers attempt to explain, *and yet perfectly One; not exactly Three but yet Three, too!* No wonder it took us three centuries to even find a word to describe such a nonsensical image of God. Note this for now: the principle of one is lonely; the principle of two is oppositional and moves you toward preference; the principle of three is inherently moving, dynamic, and generative.

---

28. See Deuteronomy 6:4.

In our efforts to explain Trinity, we tried the shamrock; we tried three faces on one person; we tried water, ice, and steam. We tried everything we could to try to resolve what is called the "first philosophical problem" of *the one and the many*. By the fourth century, the Cappadocian Fathers (Gregory of Nyssa, Basil of Caesarea, and Gregory Nazianzen) and other mystics felt they had come to a resolution of the problem; this inspired the creation of a new language that has lasted to this day.

In effect, they said, *Don't start with the One and try to make it into Three, but start with the Three and see that this is the deepest nature of the One.* This starting point, along with the contemplative mind to understand it, was much more emphasized and developed in the Eastern church, which is frankly why it still sounds foreign to most of the Western churches.

All we know experientially is the flow itself. The drama was set in motion and has never stopped. The principle of three became the operative principle of the universe, and it undercut all dualistic thinking. Its full, cataclysmic implications are still slow in breaking into history.[29]

God is not *a* being among other beings, but rather *Being itself* revealed for any mature seeker.[30] The God whom Jesus talks about, and includes himself in, is presented as unhindered dialogue, a totally positive and inclusive flow in one direction, and a waterwheel of outpouring love that never stops!

St. Bonaventure would later call such a God a "fountain fullness" of love. Any talk of anger in God, "wrath" in God, unforgiveness in God, or any kind of holding back whatsoever, the Cappadocian mystics would see as theologically impossible and forever undone in a Trinitarian notion of God. Nothing human can stop the flow of divine love; we cannot undo the eternal pattern even by our worst sin.

God is always winning, and God's love will win. Love does not lose, nor does God lose. You can't stop the relentless outpouring force that is the divine dance. Any retributive justice projected onto God is seen through the lens of outpouring Trinity as undone by God's mercy, and is reframed

29. See Cynthia Bourgeault, *The Holy Trinity and the Law of Three: Discovering the Radical Truth at the Heart of Christianity* (Boston: Shambhala, 2013).
30. See Acts 17:28.

rightly as restorative justice, as taught by all the major prophets and many of the minor ones, too.

The Trinitarian revelation was supposed to change everything, but very few Christians allowed themselves to experience this cleansing flow.

THE RELATIONSHIP IS THE VEHICLE

Why do we get so hung up on divine math problems? At the risk of being a little abstract, let me give you my interpretation of how we got into this problem. We owe a great deal of our Western thinking to one wonderful, brilliant man called Aristotle. It's amazing how one human being could have put together the foundations for what became so many of the structures of Western thought.

Aristotle taught that there were ten different qualities to all things. I'm not going to list all ten of them; two will suffice. He said there was "substance" and there was "relationship." What defined substance was that it was independent of all else—so a tree is a substance, whereas "father" is a relationship. Do you understand the distinction he's drawing?

"Son" is also a relationship, whereas stone is a substance. Now, Aristotle ranked substance the highest. This is typical Greek thinking. Substance is that which is "independent" of all else and can stand on its own. It isn't an adjective; it's a noun. Nouns are higher than adjectives.

So what the West found itself doing in the earliest traditions, by the second and third century CE, was trying to build on Aristotle to prove that this God whom we had come to understand as Trinitarian was a substance. We didn't want an ephemeral old *relationship* God, you know. We wanted a *substantial* God whom we could prove was as good as anybody else's God! (We Catholics did the same thing with our unfortunate definition of the *transubstantiation* of the bread and wine at the Mass.)

Yet when this Jesus is revealed to us Christians by calling himself the Son of the Father and yet one with the Father, he is giving clear primacy to *relationship*. Who you are is who you are in the Father, as he would put it.[31] That is your meaning.

---

31. See John 17, among many other passages in Scripture.

"My self is God, nor is any other self known to me except my God," Catherine of Genoa said.[32]

We're not of independent substance; we exist only in relationship. How countercultural! To the Western mind, relationship always looked like second or third best: "Who wants to just be a relationship? I want to be a self-made man."

Unfortunately, this doesn't end with Aristotle. This Western hyper-individualism lays down deep roots in Latin, or Western, Christianity. Augustine comes along in the fourth and fifth centuries, describing Trinity as God in three substances united as one. By the next century, God is one substance who happens to have three relationships. Aquinas comes along in the thirteenth century saying that God is one substance, but the relationships (and he's getting closer) constitute the very nature of that substance. Ah, that's about it. He called it subsistent relationship.

Now we are prepared to say that God is not, nor does God need to be, "substance" in that historic Aristotelian sense of something independent of all else but, in fact, God is relationship itself.

And don't you see that? Have you ever met a holy person? They're always people who can stay in relationship at all costs.

People who are toxic, psychopathic, or sociopathic are always those who cannot maintain relationships, who cannot sustain relationships. They run from them. Usually, either they are loners or they make all relating with them very difficult. Surely you know ten such people.

I once met a psychiatrist who made a statement to me that I thought at first was an overstatement. He's older than I am, and he said, "Richard, at the end of your life, you'll realize that every mentally ill person you've ever worked with is basically lonely."

"Oh, come on, that's a little glib, isn't it?" I replied.

"Oh, I admit, there are probably physical reasons for some mental illness, but loneliness is what activates it."

---

32. Saint Catherine of Genoa, in *Life and Doctrine of Saint Catherine of Genoa*, ed. Paul A. Boar Sr. (Veritatis Splendor Publications, 2012), 59. This is a reedited version of the work by the same title published in 1907 by Christian Press Association Publishing Company.

I've run this theory by several psychiatrist friends. After they get over their initial stunned objection—"Oh, come on. That's too simple"—they agree! Every case of nonphysiologically-based mental illness stems from a person who has been separated, cut off, living alone, forgetting how to relate. This person does not know intimacy and is starved for communion.

That's probably why God created the sexual drive so strong in most of us. It's an instinct that demands relationship in its healthy manifestation, because when you separate yourself from others you become sick, toxic, and—I'm going to say—even evil.

I think we're back again to this mystery of Trinity. Now we're prepared to say that God is absolute relatedness. I would name *salvation* as simply the readiness, the capacity, and the willingness to stay in relationship.

As long as you show up, the Spirit will keep working. That's why Jesus shows up in this world as a naked, vulnerable one—a defenseless baby. Talk about utter relationship! Naked vulnerability means I'm going to let you influence me; I'm going to allow you to change me.

What's the alternative?

"You can't change me."

"You can't teach me anything."

"I know already."

"I have all the answers."

Trump?

When you don't give other people any power in your life, when you block them, I think you're spiritually dead. And not far from evil.

It won't be long before you start doing evil things. Oh sure, you won't *call* them evil—you will not even recognize them as evil on the surface of your awareness. Atomized, sequestered consciousness is the seed of unrelated Aristotelian independence bearing its full fruit in Western isolation; we become unquestioned masters of our own shrinking kingdoms. Empathy starves in those hermetically sealed containers of self; goodness goes there to die.

What a contrast to the Way of Jesus, which is an invitation to a Trinitarian way of living, loving, and relating—on earth as it is in Godhead.

We—not you, but *we*—are intrinsically like the Trinity, living in an absolute relatedness.

We call this *love*.

We really were made for love, and outside of it we die very quickly.

And our spiritual lineage tells us that Love is personal—"*God is love.*"[33]

Now let's try to convince you that this being whom we call God is, in fact, loving. We haven't had very good success at this, right? In my decades of priesthood, I've observed that the vast majority of Christians are afraid of God. In my now broad and worldwide experience, I do not find most Christians to be naturally more loving than those of other faiths. We just think we are! It's rather disappointing to find this out, but it's inevitable if you're basically relating to this God out of fear and if your religion is, by and large, fire insurance just in case the whole thing turns out to be real.

You're not really in this dance. You haven't crawled into bed to sleep between your divine Parents.

Now do you see why we picture the Holy Spirit as a dove or as the wind? You can't capture that as easily, can you?

The best we could do was metaphor.

Once more, all religious language is metaphor—I hope you know that. It's the best we can do. We're like blind people touching the side of an elephant, describing the tiny portion we feel with all the conviction we can muster.

But the Spirit was always the hardest to describe, and even Jesus acknowledges this: *The Spirit blows where it will;*[34] don't try to control the Spirit by saying where the Spirit comes from, where the Spirit goes, or who definitely "has" the Spirit. God has many that the churches do not have, and the churches have many that God does not have.

METAPHORS BE WITH YOU!   *metaphor = to carry across*

The Greek root of the word *metaphor* means "to carry across" a meaning—to get from one place to another. The paradox is, all metaphors by

---

33. It's right here in our Bibles! See 1 John 4:8, 16.
34. See John 3:8.

necessity walk with a limp. And yet, metaphors carry a substantial—and needed—load. I offer you the wisdom of the Canadian writer Donald Braun, who says at the beginning of his book *The Journey from Ennuied*, "That which is belittled in plain speech finds the respect it warrants in the subtleties of metaphor."[35]

So metaphor is the only possible language available to us when we speak of God, and surely when we dare to speak of the mystery of Trinity. We have already begun to speak metaphorically about the "circle dance." Let's try another image:

> God is like a rubber band.

Years ago, I was in a hotel room preparing for a major conference where I was asked to reflect on the life of God as Trinity. I found myself sharing what is essentially the book you're holding.

Before I left my room that day, I prayed, *Okay God, I want to say something that is somehow true and even compelling. Please keep me out of the way.* At the end of the prayer, I looked down on the floor, and at the bottom of the bedstead I saw an ordinary rubber band; there it was, on an otherwise clean rug, glaring at me. They should have cleaned the room that morning, but I have to believe it was there for a reason. I left the room in confidence, knowing I had a new and helpful metaphor for what I wanted to say.

When I pull a rubber band outward, a centrifugal force is created; I expand my fingers and the rubber band stretches with them. And soon, an opposite motion occurs—the very thing that pulls the rubber band outward (in this case my thumb and index finger) finds itself included within it. A centripetal force then acts to pull what is included back to the center. It's one complete motion—moving out and allowing oneself to be pulled back in.

Now remember, in the New Testament, no one used the word *Trinity*. It wasn't until the third century that Tertullian (150–240), sometimes called "the founder of Western Christian theology," first coined this word *Trinity* from the Latin *trinitas*, meaning "triad," or *trinus*, meaning "three-fold." Again, the word itself is not found in the Bible; it took history awhile to find a proper word for this always-elusive "rubber band."

---

35. Donald Braun, *The Journey from Ennuied* (Victoria, BC, Canada: FriesenPress, 2015), v.

But this doesn't mean the experience itself wasn't present from the earliest days of the Christian era. Already in the New Testament, we have Jesus addressing his God—who is apparently other than himself—and we have Jesus offering to share a part of himself, also the Father's self, which he calls *Spirit*.

Father, Son, Spirit: *Which is which?* our ancestors surely wondered. Jesus describes this full flow in and out as *breathing*,[36] which is yet another good metaphor, *breath* and *Spirit* being linguistically inseparable in Hebrew. Thus, the *holy breath* emanates from God and is named as God.

These multiple namings of divinity were very confusing for many readers of the Gospels, and even are to this day. I'm amazed that John's early gospel speaks so readily and with seeming ease in this direction—both from and to Jewish monotheists, at that! How did we arrive at such a mystical ability to speak with almost no precedents in this regard? And with such quiet confidence? Only if there was deep inner experience of the same.

We see that even Jesus is looking for metaphors, for possible language to try to describe his own inner dynamic. We can find, hiding in plain sight, his natural and lovely way of knowing reality—passed on to his earliest apprentices and, by extension, to us.

A MIRRORED UNIVERSE *Participatory Knowledge*

Like probably nothing else, all authentic knowledge of God is *participatory knowledge*. I must say this directly and clearly because it is a very different way of knowing reality—and it should be the unique, open-horizoned gift of people of faith. But we ourselves have almost entirely lost this way of knowing, ever since the food fights of the Reformation and the rationalism of the Enlightenment, leading to fundamentalism on the Right and atheism or agnosticism on the Left.

Neither of these know how to know! We have sacrificed our unique telescope for a very inadequate microscope.

Divine knowing—some would call it spiritual intuition—is actually an allowing of someone else to know in us, through us, for us, and even *as* us. It demands what I often call an "identity transplant."

---

36. See, for example, John 20:21–22.

1 Corinthians 1:17-2:16

This isn't some New Age idea! Esteemed sixteenth-century teacher, Carmelite friar, and priest John of the Cross describes this Trinitarian transplant this way:

> One should not think it impossible that the soul be capable of so sublime an activity as this breathing in God, through participation as God breathes in her. For, granted that God favors her by union with the Most Blessed Trinity, in which she becomes deiform and God through participation, how could it be incredible that she also understand, know, and love—or better that this be done in her—in the Trinity, together with it, as does the Trinity itself! Yet God accomplishes this in the soul through communication and participation. This is transformation in the three Persons in power and wisdom and love, and thus the soul is like God through this transformation. He created her in His image and likeness that she might attain such resemblance.[37]

Such knowing does not inflate the ego but beautifully humbles it, teaching us patience, because even a little bit of spiritual knowing goes a long way. Read Paul's *Sermo Sapientiae* (Sermon on Wisdom) in 1 Corinthians 1:17–2:16 if you want to be exposed to a masterful attempt to describe this alternative way of knowing. It is, frankly, why the gifts of the Spirit distinguish between knowledge and wisdom,[38] which most of us think are the same thing. Spiritual knowing is often called *wisdom,* and must be distinguished from merely having correct information or knowledge.

In other words, God (and uniquely the Trinity) cannot be known as we know any other object—such as a machine, an objective idea, or a tree—which we are able to "objectify." We look at objects, and we judge them from a distance through our normal intelligence, parsing out their varying parts, separating this from that, presuming that to understand the parts is always to be able to understand the whole. But divine things can never be objectified in this way; they can only be "subjectified" by becoming one

---

37. St. John of the Cross, "The Spiritual Canticle," stanza 39, commentary, no. 4, in *The Collected Works of St. John of the Cross,* trans. Kieran Kavanaugh, O.C.D. and Otilio Rodriguez, O.C.D. (Washington, DC: ICS [Institute of Carmelite Studies] Publications, 1973), 558. Translation of *Obras de San Juan de la Cruz.* Reprint; previously published in 1964 by Doubleday.
38. See Isaiah 11:2; 1 Corinthians 12:8.

with them! *When neither yourself nor the other is treated as a mere object, but both rest in an I-Thou of mutual admiration, you have spiritual knowing.*[39] Some of us call this contemplative knowing.

Such knowing intuits things in their wholeness, with all levels of connection and meaning, and perhaps how they fit in the full scheme of things. Thus, the contemplative response to the moment is always appreciation and inherent *re-spect* ("to look at a second time") because I am now a part of what I am trying to see. Our first practical and partial observation of most things lacks this respect. It is not yet *contemplative* knowing. Frankly, *when you see things contemplatively, everything in the universe is a mirror!* How seriously I mean this will become clear as we proceed.

Now just hold on to this, dear readers, because the originating mystery of Trinity both names and begins the mirroring process, allowing us to know all that we need to know by the same endless process of mirroring and reflecting.[40] We know things in their depth and beauty only by this second gaze of love.

Hold on to this central metaphor of mirroring as we move forward: a true mirror first receives an image and then reflects it back truthfully—but now so that I can see myself, too. The all-important thing is that you find the right mirror that mirrors you honestly and at depth. All personhood is created in this process, and our job is always to stay inside this mirroring. This is almost exactly what Heinz Kohut, the psychoanalyst, was saying with his "self psychology."[41] Here we are saying that the same is true theologically and spiritually; our task is to trustfully receive and then reflect back the inner image transmitted to us until, as the apostle Paul expressed, "we are gradually turned into the image that we reflect."[42]

This is the whole spiritual journey in one sentence! All love, goodness, and holiness is a reflected gift. You take all things into yourself by gazing at them with reverence, and this completes the circuit of love—because this is how creation is looking out at you. The inner life of the Trinity has become the outer life of all creation. This is good!

39. See Martin Buber, *I and Thou* (New York: Scribner, 1958).
40. See 2 Corinthians 3:18; Romans 1:20.
41. See, for example, Heinz Kohut, *Self Psychology and the Humanities* (New York: W. W. Norton & Co., Inc., 1985).
42. See 2 Corinthians 3:18.

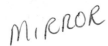

This is all about expanding our recognition and reverence for the universal mystery of Incarnation (the enfleshment of the Divine) until, in the end, as Augustine shockingly puts it, "there shall be one Christ, loving Himself."[43] And of course, he is only building on Paul: "*There is only Christ: he is everything and he is in everything.*"[44] The Christ is the universalization of what many of us first fell in love with in Jesus. But this deserves a whole other book,[45] and I am jumping ahead of ourselves. But I do want you to know where this is all going—and where it came from. The divine mirroring will never stop; mirroring is how the whole transformation process is personally initiated and finally achieved.

But we have to be taught how to "gaze steadily into this law of perfect freedom, and make this our habit," as James so brilliantly intuits it.[46]

Jesus comes forth from the infinite life of the Trinity and invites us and includes us back in the Infinitely Receiving Gaze so that now we can have participatory knowledge of the same,[47] because no objectification of God is ever possible. We can only be mirrored, and we can only know and see ourselves fully both in a mirror and through a mirror. It is thus crucial and central to have a well-polished mirror that can see and reflect God in you. Yes, good theology and God-image are important!

And dare we believe that God sees a bit of Godself mirrored in new form as God gazes at us? This is a very fair conclusion.

Mirrored knowledge is not "logical" knowledge—it's *reflected* and *received* knowledge. That's why it's difficult to prove God or to prove love to anybody who hasn't been in the receiving line itself. In fact, it's largely impossible. Note how Moses' face *shines* after he's received the divine gaze and been seen truthfully and lovingly,[48] and yet he always covers it with a veil when he goes among the people. This is no small symbol. All people

43. St. Augustine, "Ten Homilies on the First Epistle of John," trans. H. Browne, in *Nicene and Post-Nicene Fathers of the Christian Church*, vol. 7, ed. Philip Schaff, rev. Joseph H. Myers (New York: The Christian Literature Company, 1888), 521.
44. Colossians 3:11.
45. Thankfully, I've already partly written it! See my book *Eager to Love* (Cincinnati, OH: Franciscan Media, 2014), app. I, 209.
46. See James 1:25.
47. See John 14:3, 18–20.
48. See Exodus 34:29–35.

need to be seen for themselves and as themselves, and receive the divine gaze intimately—and not just rely on someone else's seeing.

Three times, Scripture mentions that Moses was the only one who knew YHWH "*face to face.*"[49] This is the first account of the divine unveiling in the biblical tradition, and it is done precisely through a process of personal *interface*, or mirroring. The image is effectively transferred to Moses, and then he spends the rest of his life trying to pass on the mirroring to the wandering Israelites—with scant success. People prefer laws and reassuring repetitive rituals to intimate mirroring. True mirroring only needs to be received and recognized once—and once is enough to change you forever. But it deepens if we "gaze steadily and make it a habit," as James says. This is the heart of all prayer.

It is very hard to talk about spiritual things in a totally objective or external way. It's very hard to talk about inner experience because, frankly, if you haven't been there, you haven't been there. If you don't desire to mirror others, you probably haven't been effectively mirrored yourself. And the Divine Mirror is what James calls "*the perfect law of freedom*"[50] because it reflects us with a totally liberating love and acceptance. Perhaps one of the greatest weaknesses of institutional religion is that we've given people the impression that the pope could know for us, or the experts could know for us, or the Bible could know for us—that we could have second-hand knowledge of holy things, and could be really invested in the sacred because someone else told us it was true. God ended up being an outer "thing" and largely remained *out there*, extraneous to the experience of the soul, the heart, and even the transformed mind. Yet God has no grandchildren, only children.

Holy Spirit

Thus, we tried to know God through objectified knowledge, which finally became a boring facsimile of knowledge because we weren't in on the deal; it was literally outside us and beyond us. This is much of organized religion.

Humans get excited about something only if it includes them in some way. God surely knew this about us, and so God included us inside of God's own knowing—by planting the Holy Spirit within us as the Inner Knower

49. Exodus 33:11; Numbers 12:8; Deuteronomy 34:10.
50. James 1:25.

and Reminder of "all things."[51] This is indeed a *re-minding*, a very different kind of mind that is given to us!

But it gets even better: we know and accept ourselves in the very same movement in which we're knowing and accepting God; in surrendering to God, we simultaneously accept our best and fullest self. What a payoff! What a truly holy exchange! And it's all accomplished in the process of mirroring. On the psychological level, this is Heinz Kohut's "recovery of the self."[52]

The doctrine of Trinity says that it's finally participatory knowledge that matters, not rational calculating, which is but one limited form of knowing. God—and the human person by an irreducibly important extension—must never be objectified. In fact, God refuses to be an object of our thinking. As John of the Cross so frequently insisted, God refuses to be known but can only be loved.[53]

Here is the sad tradeoff that most Western believers have settled for: science is allowed to give us the big field of objective and helpful knowledge, and religion is allowed to give us the smaller subjective field of personally meaningful wisdom. Cynthia Bourgeault, who teaches in our Living School at the Center for Action and Contemplation, rightly calls this "crazy-making."[54] We both agree it is at the heart of our anemic and split-mind Christianity, which mass-produces both fundamentalists and practical agnostics inside the church—and sincere atheists outside it. What a shame and what a loss. In fact, true spirituality should give us access to the bigger field, but it does not seem that most of our religions have risen above the tribal level up to now. Perhaps we have been lacking Trinity!

---

51. See John 14:26.

52. See Heinz Kohut, *The Restoration of the Self* (Madison, CT: International Universities Press, 1977). This work (and most of Kohut's other books) develops the concept of mirroring as basic to the formation of self, both positively and negatively. We need "self objects" that narcissistically mirror us back to ourselves, or we cannot begin to know who we are. This is called the "mirror transference." We initially and necessarily "use" others so that we can ironically stop using others—and can freely pass on the mirroring to others, instead. A seeming paradox! Schizophrenics often stare in mirrors for extended periods trying to mirror themselves to themselves, presumably because they never received proper mirroring from another. It does not work to heal them; correct and perfect mirroring is achieved in the Trinity.

53. See, for example, David Benner, *Surrender to Love* (Downers Grove, IL: InterVarsity Press, 2003), 29.

54. Bourgeault, *Law of Three*, 208.

> *God can only be loved and enjoyed, which ironically ends up being its own new kind of knowing.* This is absolutely central and pivotal.

Now, if the very nature of this God is a centrifugal force flowing outward that becomes a centripetal force drawing inward (similar to a rubber band, or as in mirroring), then we'd have every right to expect a *family resemblance* between ourselves and everything else. Trinity allows our scientific and spiritual cosmologies to finally operate as one, which we had best discover very quickly before the divide deepens or appears unbridgeable.

If a loving Creator started this whole thing, then there has to be a "DNA connection," as it were, between the One who creates and what is created. One of the many wonderful things that scientists are discovering as they compare their observations through microscopes with those through telescopes is that the pattern of the neutrons, protons, and atoms is similar to the pattern of planets, stars, and galaxies: both are in orbit, and all is relational to everything else. We now know the same is true in biology, as Robert Lanza's work on biocentrism so brilliantly demonstrates: "the universe is created by life and not the other way around."[55] Life-flow is the ground of everything, absolutely everything.

There is a similarity between the perceived two ends of the universe, the Divine and the human, just as we should have expected: "Let *us* create in *our* own image, in the likeness of *ourselves*" is how Genesis first described the Creator speaking.[56] And the Hebrew even uses the plural pronouns for some wonderful reason.

The Jewish intuition was there from the beginning. They didn't have scientific evidence for it yet; it was just simple interface with the world. Spiritual *intuitions* are almost always on some level correct. It's what we do with them when we literalize them and make them wooden, mechanical, and fundamentalist that causes them to lose the *flow*, and the flow is exactly where the life is at.

What could have been a Divine Wave, we have for the most part related to as a static particle god.

---

55. See http://www.robertlanza.com/the-biocentric-universe-theory-life-creates-time-space-and-the-cosmos-itself/.
56. See Genesis 1:26.

This demotion made a whole bunch of Christian dogmas appear to be believing in magic—purely transactional and almost always for an exclusive few. Our "good news" was no longer *catholic*, or universal, truth but merely ethnic, cultural, and earthbound truth.

We have a lot of catching up to do.

The energy in the universe is not in the planets, or in the protons or neutrons, but in *the relationship between them*. Not in the particles but in the space between them. Not in the cells of organisms but in the way the cells feed and give feedback to one another. Not in any precise *definition* of the three persons of the Trinity as much as in the *relationship between the Three*! This is where all the power for infinite renewal is at work:

The loving relationship between them.

The infinite love between them.

The dance itself.

In other words, it is an entirely relational universe. If, at any time, we try to stop this flow moving *through* us, *with* us, and *in* us,[57] we fall into the true state of sin—and it is truly a state more than a momentary behavior.

Sin is the state of being closed down, shut off, blocked, and thus resisting the eternal flow that we're meant to be. By a hardened heart or a cold spirit, by holding another person apart in hatred, you've thus cut *yourself* off from the flow. Jesus therefore criticizes the religious leaders who want to condemn the woman caught in adultery much more than the woman herself. Jesus' words to the murderous, religious bean counters in John 8 forever stand as a rather wholesale critique of all stone-throwing, and they locate sin where we would rather not see it.

The divine flow either flows both in and out, or it is not flowing at all. The Law of Flow is simple, and Jesus states it in many formulations, such as "Happy are the merciful; they shall have mercy shown to them."[58]

Sin is always a refusal of mutuality and a closing down into separateness. In his classic *The Great Divorce*, C. S. Lewis has the soul in hell

---

57. Notice that these are the same three prepositions that we use at the end of the Eucharistic Prayer ("through him, and with him, and in him"), to which the community responds with the great "Amen!"

58. See Matthew 5:7 (JB).

Separation / Closed off

shouting out, "*I don't want help. I want to be left alone.*"[59] Whenever we refuse mutuality toward anything...whenever we won't allow our deep inner-connectedness to guide us...whenever we're not attuned to both receiving and giving, you could say that the Holy Spirit is existentially absent from our lives. (Not *essentially*, however.)

This is indeed the "sin against the Holy Spirit" that "cannot be forgiven,"[60] only because it does not look like one of those naughty things that needs forgiveness! And so we'd never think of even asking for forgiveness, smugly sitting over there in our self-complacent corner. True evil and true sin must be very well disguised to survive. Separation will normally not look like sin, but will often resemble propriety and even appropriate boundary-keeping. "I have a right to be upset!" the righteous soul says. No one ever "deserves" our kindness; in fact, what makes it kindness is that you are not even asking that silly question.

VULNERABILITY

Did you ever imagine that what we call "vulnerability" might just be the key to ongoing growth? In my experience, healthily vulnerable people use every occasion to expand, change, and grow. Yet it is a risky position to live undefended, in a kind of constant openness to the other—because it would mean others could sometimes actually wound you (from *vulnus*, "wound"). But only if we choose to take this risk do we also allow the exact opposite possibility: the other might also gift you, free you, and even love you.

But it is a felt risk every time.

Every time.

If and when we can live such a vulnerable life, without ceasing—the life we see mirrored in a God who is described as three persons perfectly handing over, emptying themselves out, and then fully receiving what has been handed over—there will always be a centrifugal force flowing through, out, and beyond us. Inside Trinity, a spiritual life simply becomes "the imitation of God,"[61] as impossible as this sounds to our ordinary levels of abiding and awareness.

59. C S. Lewis, *The Great Divorce* (New York: HarperCollins, 2001), 59. Emphasis added.
60. See Matthew 12:31–32; Luke 12:10.
61. See Ephesians 5:1.

This, then, seems to be the work of the Spirit: to keep you growing is to keep you vulnerable to life and love itself. Notice that the major metaphors for the Spirit are always dynamic, energetic, and moving: elusive wind, descending dove, falling fire, and flowing water. Spirit-led people never stop growing and changing and recognizing the new moment of opportunity. How strange to think that so much of religion became a worship of the status quo, until you remember that the one thing the ego hates and fears more than anything else is change.

What, then, is the path to holiness? It's the same as the path to wholeness. And we are never "there" yet. We are always just *in the river.*

Don't try to push the river or make the river happen; it is already happening, and you cannot stop it. All you can do is recognize it, enjoy it, and ever more fully allow it to carry you.

This is the great surprise, and for some a disappointment: this divine flow has very little to do with you.

As the late Irish poet and priest John O'Donohue put it:

I would love to live
Like a river flows,
Carried by the surprise
Of its own unfolding.[62]

The flow doesn't have to do with you being perfect. It doesn't have to do with you being right. Nor is it ever about belonging to the right group. You do not even have to understand it. How could you? You have surely noticed that Jesus never has any such checklist test before he heals anybody. He just says, as it were, "Are you going to allow yourself to be touched? If so, let's go!"

The touchable ones are the healed ones; it's pretty much that simple. There's no doctrinal test. There's no moral test. There is no checking out if they are Jewish, gay, baptized, or in their first marriage. There's only the one question:

Do you want to be healed?

---

62. John O'Donohue, "Fluent," *Conamara Blues* (New York: Cliff Street Books, 2001), 23.

If the answer is a vulnerable, trusting, or confident one, the flow always happens, and the person is healed. Try to disprove me on that!

And believe it or not, it's much harder to allow this touch and to surrender to this flow than it is to have a strong moral stance on this or that, or to believe doctrines about this, that, or the other, which is surely why the unconverted person falls to these lower levels instead of just staying trustfully in the always-vulnerable river of life.

WEAK WISDOM

Let's stay with this matter of vulnerability for a moment, and even its less-flattering synonym: *weakness*.

"Weak" isn't a trait any of us wish to be associated with, and yet the apostle Paul describes no less than *God* having weakness! Paul says that *"God's weakness is stronger than human strength."*[63] How could God be weak? We are in a new ballpark here.

Let's admit that we admire strength and importance. We admire self-sufficiency, autonomy, the self-made person. This is surely the American way. This weakness of God, as Paul calls it, is not something we admire or want to imitate.

Maybe this has been part of our resistance to this mystery of Trinity.

Human strength I would describe as self-sufficiency.

God's weakness I would describe as inter-being.

Inter-being is a different way of standing in the world than the self-made person stands. Human strength admires holding on. There is something positive about this; it's not all wrong. But the irony is, this mystery is much more about letting go, which looks—let's admit it—first of all like weakness to us, not like strength.

We're almost embarrassed by this mystery of Trinity; maybe that's why we haven't unpackaged it.

Human strength admires autonomy; God's mystery rests in mutuality.

---

63. 1 Corinthians 1:25.

We like control; God, it seems, loves vulnerability. In fact, if Jesus is the image of God, then God is much better described as "Absolute Vulnerability Between Three" than "All-mighty One." Yet how many Christian prayers begin with some form of "Almighty God"? If you're immersed in the Trinitarian mystery, you must equally say "All-Vulnerable God," too!

But Brené Brown's popularity notwithstanding,[64] vulnerability isn't admired in our culture, is it? Could a truly vulnerable candidate easily be elected president of the United States? I doubt it. It seems like a prerequisite to appear like you know more than you really do; this impresses us for some reason. If we haven't touched and united with the vulnerable place within us, we're normally projecting seeming invulnerability outside. This seems to be particularly true of men, as many years of giving male initiation rites taught me.[65]

Human strength wants to promote, project, and protect a clear sense of self-identity and autonomy and not inter-being or interface.

"I know who I am," we love to say. And yet we have this Father, Son, and Holy Spirit operating out of a *received* identity given by another. "I am Son only in relationship to Father, and he gives me my who-ness, my being."

We admire needing no one; apparently, the Trinity admires needing.

Needing everything—total communion with all things and all being (although *needing* may be in a metaphorical sense). We're practiced at hiding and self-protecting, not at showing all our cards. God seems to be into total disclosure.

---

64. What? You haven't read or watched any of Brené Brown's wonderful research and teaching about vulnerability? Find your way to brenebrown.com immediately!

65. The initiation of young males, usually between the ages of 13–17, was the absolute norm in almost all indigenous cultures on all continents until this began to fall apart in the last couple of centuries. Here was the universal assumption: If the male is not *made* to walk journeys of powerlessness, you can assume he will almost always abuse any power that he attains. Such individualism and power-seeking was toxic for the survival of any tribe or community. Thus, "rites of passage" assured at least some degree of humility, vulnerability, interiority, and spirituality in the male, who usually avoids all of these if he possibly can. Today, the male initiation community I cofounded continues to flourish as Illuman (Illuman.org). See also the worldwide ManKind Project (ManKindProject.org) and its women's corollary, Woman Within (WomanWithin.org).

Human strength is defined in asserting boundaries. God, it seems, is in the business of dissolving boundaries. So we enter into paradox—what's Three is one and what's One is three. We just can't resolve that, and so we confuse unity with uniformity.

God endlessly creates and allows diversity. All you need to do is look at the animal world, the world under the sea, hidden little insects, or all the human beings in a grocery store—who of you looks alike?

God clearly loves diversity. In all creation, is there any evidence to show that God is into uniformity? We like it because it gives the ego a sense of control—a false one. And so we constantly substitute uniformity for unity, obedience for love, and conformity for true loyalty to our deepest identity—which takes much more confidence and courage.

The mystery that we're talking about here is clearly diversity on display! The Three are diverse, different, and distinct—and yet they are one. What is it *about* this diversity that's so intrinsic to Trinity's DNA? Read on.

THE DELIGHT OF DIVERSITY

One of the most wonderful things I find in this naming of God as Father, Son, and Holy Spirit is its affirmation that there is an *intrinsic plurality* to goodness. Just hold on to that, all right?

Goodness isn't *sameness*. Goodness, to be goodness, needs contrast and tension, not perfect uniformity. If Father, Son, and Holy Spirit are all God yet clearly different, and we embrace this differentiation, resisting the temptation to blend them into some kind of amorphous blob, then there are *at least* three shapes to pure goodness. (And of course, probably more.)

God's goal, it seems to me, is the same in creation. It is the making of persons, not the making of a uniform mob, which means there is clear diversity and a kind of what I'm going to call open-endedness in all of nature, and to the very nature of this creation. In other words, heaven is precisely not uniformity. Because we did not honor Trinity, many Christians were totally unprepared for any notion of evolution—again forcing many would-be believers into quite sincere atheism.

The diversity of heaven was never something I considered in my earlier years. I thought we were all handed the same white robe and standard-issue harp, assigned to an identical cloud for all eternity.

But how does Jesus deconstruct this big-box, strip-mall, McHeaven franchise? He tells us: *"In my Father's house are many mansions."*[66]

What a contrast! Even in the eternal nature of things, you're somehow *you* in your you-ness, on the path that God is leading *you* on, the journey *you* are going through, the burdens that *you* are bearing. All of these are combining to create the precise alchemy of *your* soul, *your* holiness, and *your* response. In the eternal scheme of things, we discover that all God wants from you is *you.*

It's just so humbling, because it always feels like not enough, doesn't it?

"All I want to do is be like Saint Francis," I said to my spiritual director, over and over, for my first decade as a Franciscan.

Finally, one day, he said, "Hey Richard, you're not, and you're never going to be, Francis of Assisi. You're not even close, all right? You're 'unfortunately' Richard Rohr from Kansas." I said to myself, *This doesn't sound nearly as dramatic or exciting.*

Except when I realized: all God wants is Richard from Kansas.

But that's what I don't know how to give you, God!

It feels so insignificant, and yet this is the liberating secret: I am precisely the gift God wants—in full and humble surrender. There is unity between the path taken and the destination where we finally arrive. Saints are not uniform but are each unique creations of grace according to the journey God has led them through.

This is God's great risk of freedom: allowing us the freedom to do our own thing. The scandal of grace is that God will even defer—talk about self-emptying!—to using these mistaken dead ends in our favor. This is the ultimate turnaround of love: each of us is our own beauty, a freely-created, grace-sculpted beauty—what poets and dramatists often name *tragic beauty.*

Don't feel bad about this. Look at the cross.

---

66. See John 14:2 (NKJV, KJV).

Is that not a tragic beauty? Is that not what we are?

That we've come to God through tragedy, not by doing things right but invariably by doing things wrong, is a gift. We've learned so much more by our mistakes than we ever have by our successes.

In the men's rite of passage work that I've done, I tell the men on the last night before initiation that success has nothing—absolutely nothing—to teach you spiritually after age thirty. It just feels good. That's all. Everything you learn at my age—in my seventies now—is by failure, humiliation, and suffering; things falling apart. Dissolution is the only thing that allows the soul to go to a deeper place.

So why do I dare say this is true and not fear that you're going to call me some cheap secular humanist? How do I know that this quixotic, winding-road character of holiness is not just my wishful thinking?

Precisely because of this Trinity code. It reveals a pattern of perfect freedom in relationship whereby each person allows the other to be themselves, and yet remains in perfect given-ness toward the other, not withholding from other-ness.

Contemporary Franciscan, scholar, and teacher Ilia Delio asks if we can reframe our entire understanding of God, freedom, and relationship along evolutionary, Trinitarian lines:

> Can we understand the Trinity as an infinite emergent process? In this respect, change is not contrary to God; rather, change is integral to God because God is love and love is constantly transcending itself toward greater union.... The dynamic life of the Trinity as ever newness in love means that every divine relationship is a new beginning because every divine person is a transcendent horizon of love. Being is transcendence in love, and God's Being in love is eternally free.[67]

Here we find the pattern that allows us to create authentic community and authentic unity, celebrating authentic freedom. I know those of us who are Americans love this word *freedom*, but I don't think we understand it in its full-blown spiritual sense, which asks much more of us than,

67. Ilia Delio, *The Emergent Christ* (Maryknoll, NY: Orbis Books, 2011), 4–5.

for example, protecting boundaries from terrorists. True spiritual freedom is only attained, as far as I can see, by one who sleeps and rests inside God's perfect freedom. Diversity is created and maintained in Trinitarian love. Freedom is created and maintained in Trinitarian love. Union is not destroyed by diversity or by freedom.

THE WORLD IN A WORD

A Trinitarian person who is in formation is someone being freed of narcissism's chains. A partner in the divine dance is someone who agrees to stand in the mutual relationship that *God is*—the relationship that God has already drawn us into gratuitously.

As Lay Cistercian and teacher Carl McColman puts it:

> God is in us, because we are in Christ. As members of the mystical body, Christians actually partake in the divine nature of the Trinity. We do not merely *watch* the dance, we *dance* the dance. We join hands with Christ and the Spirit flows through us and between us and our feet move always in the loving embrace of the Father. In that we are members of the mystical body of Christ, we see the joyful love of the Father through the eyes of the Son. And with every breath, we breathe the Holy Spirit.[68]

But hand-taking, embracing, and breathing-with aren't often immediately attractive to us! Vulnerability, letting go, total disclosure, surrender—these don't come easily in the cultural waters we're swimming in. Culture is built on a movement toward empire, toward aggrandizement of the group, toward making itself number one—this creates the interior conflict that Scripture already describes as the conflict between the world and the Spirit.

And please understand that in the New Testament, the oft-used word *world* doesn't refer to creation. The best interpretation would be the "system." This system is the way we structure reality, and it's almost always going to be diametrically opposed to the mystery of the Trinity. You can

---

68. Carl McColman, *The Big Book of Christian Mysticism: The Essential Guide to Contemplative Spirituality* (Charlottesville, VA: Hampton Roads Publishing Company, 2010), 165–166. Emphasis is in the original.

see why the most Jesus hoped for—and why we say you can't understand Jesus without the Trinity—is that his group become a *"little flock."*[69] Today, we call it "critical mass." The Gospels call it *"the Twelve."*[70] Jesus calls it *"leaven,"*[71] or *"yeast."*[72] He seems to have the patience and humility to trust a slow, leavening process. This is quite different from any notion of empire or "Christendom," which always relies upon the use of power.

There's no evidence Jesus ever expected his little movement to take over the world—that is, the "system"—but instead that there'd be just enough people living into this kind of mutuality to be the leaven in the dough keeping this entire creation from total delusion and self-destruction. Please don't jump to the conclusion, though, that God doesn't love (and indeed like) all those who are "in and of" the system. They just suffer from divided loyalties. That said, they can be good homing devices—sometimes much better than those of us who pretend we are outside or above the system.

And if you're truly "saved"—that is, living loved and living liberated—you know what makes this evident? It's precisely your ability to see that luminous presence everywhere else. If you can't see that, you're not very saved, in my opinion. Your seeing and allowing does not match God's. I don't care how many services you pack out. I don't care how many ministries you serve with. I don't care how many commandments you've obeyed. You're not enlightened, transformed, saved—pick your religious safety word—you still don't trust the Mystery.

But there's good news: you can give up all condemnation for Lent and leave your antagonisms in the empty tomb! The more light and goodness you can see, the more Trinitarian you are. When you can see as Jesus and my father St. Francis see, you see divine light in everyone, *especially* in those who are different, who are "other," who are sinners, wounded, lepers, and lame—in those, as Scripture seems to indicate, where God shows up the best.

Mother Teresa summed this up beautifully, in ways Eucharistic and kenotic:

---

69. See Luke 12:32.
70. See, for example, Mark 9:35.
71. See, for example, Matthew 13:33 (NKJV, KJV).
72. See, for example, Matthew 13:33.

We [the Missionaries of Charity] are called to be contemplatives in the heart of the world by:

Seeking the face of God in everything, everyone, everywhere, all the time, and seeing His hand in every happening.

Seeing and adoring the presence of Jesus, especially in the lowly appearance of bread, and in the distressing disguise of the poor.[73]

The degree to which you can see the divine image where you'd rather not tells me how fully the divine image is now operative within you.

Your life is no longer your own. You are instead a two-way reflecting mirror.

RESHAPING OUR IMAGE

Please don't begin with some notion of abstract being and then say, *Okay, we found out through Jesus that such a being is loving.*

No, Trinitarian revelation says *start with the loving—and this is the new definition of being!* There is now *a hidden faithfulness* at the heart of the universe. Everything is now positioned to transform all of our lead into gold; the final direction of history is inevitably directed toward resurrection as Alpha becomes Omega,[74] as both Bonaventure and Teilhard de Chardin would put it. This is much of what I talk about in my earlier books *Immortal Diamond* and *Eager to Love*, if you want to pursue this point further.[75]

But let's switch shapes; I know using geometrical figures sometimes helps us to think differently. Those of us who grew up with the pre-Trinitarian notion of God probably saw reality, consciously or unconsciously, as a pyramid-shaped universe, with God at the top of the triangle and all else beneath. Most Christian art and church design and architecture reflects this pyramidal worldview, which shows what little influence Trinity has had in our history.

---

73. Mother Teresa, *In the Heart of the World: Thoughts, Stories, and Prayers* (Novato, CA: New World Library, 2010), 33.
74. See Revelation 1:8; 21:6; 22:13.
75. *Immortal Diamond* (San Francisco: Jossey-Bass, 2013); *Eager to Love* (Cincinnati, OH: Franciscan Media, 2014).

I'm not saying the pyramid is entirely wrong. We certainly want to preserve a sense of transcendent greatness in God. I know that God is well beyond me, or God would not be any kind of God I could respect. But if this idea of Trinity is the shape of God, and Incarnation is true, then a more honest and truly helpful geometrical figure would be (as we have seen) a circle or even a spiral, and not a pyramid. Let the circle dance rearrange your Christian imagination. No more "old man with a white beard on a throne," please!

This Trinitarian flow is like the rise and fall of tides on a shore. *All reality can now be pictured as an Infinite Outflowing that empowers and generates an Eternal Infolding.* This eternal flow is echoed in history by the Incarnate Christ and the Indwelling Spirit. And as Meister Eckhart and other mystics say in other ways, the infolding always corresponds to the outflowing.

(I love the German word for Trinity, *Dreifaltigheit*, which literally means "the three infoldings.")

The foundational good news is that creation and humanity have been drawn into this flow! We are not outsiders or spectators[76] but inherently part of the divine dance.

Some mystics who were on real journeys of prayer took this message to its consistent conclusion: creation is thus "the fourth person of the Blessed Trinity"! Once more, the divine dance isn't a closed circle—we're all invited!

As the independent scholar, teacher, and fishing-lure designer C. Baxter Kruger puts it:

> The stunning truth is that this triune God, in amazing and lavish love, determined to open the circle and share the Trinitarian life with others. This is the one, eternal and abiding reason for the creation of the world and of human life. There is no other God, no other will of God, no second plan, no hidden agenda for human beings. Before the creation of the world, the Father, Son and Spirit set their love upon us and planned to bring us to share and know and experience the Trinitarian life itself. Unto this end the cosmos was called into being, and the human race was fashioned, and Adam and Eve were given a place in the coming of Jesus Christ,

---

76. See John 14:1–3.

the Father's Son himself, in and through whom the dream of our adoption would be accomplished.[77]

This even fits the "dynamic" metaphysical principle that "the interweaving of the three [always] produces a fourth" on another level.[78]

Sure, this may sound like heresy—especially to a contracted heart that wants to go it alone. But this is the *fourth place* pictured and reserved as a mirror in Andrei Rublev's fifteenth-century icon of the Trinity.

For those in on this open secret, their human nature has a definitive direction and dignity…a Source and a self-confidence that you just can't get in any other way. You know that your worth is not about you personally or individually doing it right on your own; instead, your humanity is just a matter of allowing and loving the divine flow, which Christians usually call the Holy Spirit.

Life becomes a matter of showing up and saying yes.

Frankly, a Trinitarian spirituality is much more of a corporate, historical, and social notion of salvation, which was always much more appreciated in the Eastern church than in the West. We will talk more about the "heresy" of Western individualism later.

Once God included us in the divine flow—both outward and inward— all we can really do is opt out, refusing to participate.[79] And sadly, that possibility must logically be preserved, or free will means nothing. And love can only thrive and expand inside of perfect freedom.[80]

ATOMIC BONDS

As I have expressed, this divine dance takes on a centripetal force, pulling the energy in, but then it becomes this centrifugal force, moving the energy out—and that is our universe: everything; no exceptions.

77. C. Baxter Kruger, *The Shack Revisited* (New York: FaithWords, 2012), 62.

78. Bourgeault, *Law of Three*, 89.

79. A reality explored both seriously and playfully in Spencer Burke and Barry Taylor's *A Heretic's Guide to Eternity* (San Francisco: Jossey-Bass, 2006).

80. See Hans Urs Von Balthasar, *Dare We Hope "That All Men Be Saved"?* (San Francisco: Ignatius Press, 1988) and David Burnfield, *Patristic Universalism*, 2nd ed. (privately published; printed by CreateSpace, Charleston, SC, 2016). These are only two of the many books that are demonstrating that the supposed heresy disparagingly called "universalism" by many Christians was a rather common belief in the early Eastern church and even the Scriptures.

Everything came forth from this divine dance, and our new appreciation of Trinity is giving us a new grounding for interfaith understanding. It's giving us a marvelous new basis for appreciating how this mystery is embedded as the code: not just in our religious constructs, but in everything that exists.

If there is only one God, and if there is one pattern to this God, then the wonderful thing is that we can expect to find that pattern everywhere. I believe one reason so many theologians are interested in Trinity right now is that we're finding quantum physics, biology, and cosmology are finally at a level of development that our understanding of everything from atoms to galaxies to organisms is affirming, confirming, and allowing us to use the old Trinitarian language, and now with a whole new level of appreciation.

A whole new level of, *"My God! It just might be true!"*

Imagine this: the deepest intuitions of our poets and mystics and Holy Writ are aligning with findings on the leading edges of science and empirical discovery. When inner and outer worlds converge like this, something beautiful is afoot—the reversal of a centuries-long lovers' quarrel between science and spirituality, mind and heart.

What physicists and contemplatives alike are confirming is that the foundational nature of reality is relational; everything is in relationship with everything else. As a central Christian mystery, we've been saying this from the very beginning while still utterly failing to grasp its meaning.

Even though, as confessional Christians, none of us would have denied the Trinitarian mystery, in essence we did. As described earlier, for all practical purposes, those of us raised Christian grew up with a monarchical God, a Pharaoh sitting at the top of a great pyramid. Right?

We grew up as functioning monarchists...while the revolution of Trinity remained humbly hidden in plain sight.

"Oh yeah, I know God is three persons, but what does that really mean?"

We reduced divine function and flow to a largely mathematical problem. What the mystics helped me understand became key for me: let go of starting with the One and then by some impossible sleight-of-hand, some *legerdemain*, trying to make God into Three.

No. Start with the Three and know that this is the only nature of the One.

Start with the mystery of relationship and relatedness; this is where the power is! It's exactly what the atomic scientists and astrophysicists are telling us today.

CREATOR AND DESTROYER OF WORLDS

Not thirty minutes from where I live in Albuquerque is the National Atomic Museum. Of the four atomic bombs that were created at Los Alamos, we dropped one just south of Albuquerque on July 16, 1945. We dropped a second one on Hiroshima, and a third one on Nagasaki. The casing of the fourth one is still right here in town. That brings this whole mystery so close to home for me—literally.

Isn't it telling, and more than interesting, that the basic building block of our entire physical universe is what we call the *atom?* And the atom is most simply understood as the orbiting structure of three particles— proton, electron, and neutron—in constant interplay with one another.

The further irony is that Robert Oppenheimer, the "father of the atom bomb," named the final stage and site of its New Mexico detonation *Trinity.* He later said that although this clear choice of name was not completely conscious to him, it was probably inspired by John Donne's metaphysical poem "Holy Sonnet #14."

Donne's meditation here invokes a kind of trinity—but is it the Trinity that we've been exploring? I'm not sure the answer is completely clear. This is a poem I find, in places, both beautiful and disturbing:

Batter my heart, three-person'd God, for you
As yet but knock, breathe, shine, and seek to mend;
That I may rise and stand, o'erthrow me, and bend
Your force to break, blow, burn, and make me new.
I, like an usurp'd town to another due,
Labor to admit you, but oh, to no end;
Reason, your viceroy in me, me should defend,
But is captiv'd, and proves weak or untrue.

Yet dearly I love you, and would be lov'd fain,
But am betroth'd unto your enemy;
Divorce me, untie or break that knot again,
Take me to you, imprison me, for I,
Except you enthrall me, never shall be free,
Nor ever chaste, except you ravish me.[81]

Such contrasting images!

As one museum dedicated to science and art noted in their reflection piece about the *Trinity* test site,

"Holy Sonnet #14" [begins,] "Batter my heart, three-personed God...." In that sonnet, the speaker addresses God directly and strong paradoxical emotions surface, all in the context of an extended warlike metaphor. Coursing through the poetry is violent imagery ("batter my heart," "overthrow me," "break, blow, burn...") paired with pleas to be healed and renewed ("seek to mend," "make me new"), evoking a sense of struggle, an internal war.[82]

When Oppenheimer was creating his bomb at Los Alamos, we were at war—as we often are. And it seems that he himself was locked in an internal battle—hoping that an instrument of death-dealing could somehow bring life; that an army, prepared to *usurp towns* themselves and inflict martial law on United States citizens, if necessary, could bring peace at home and abroad by their powers of annihilation.[83]

Perhaps the most audacious contradiction of all is Oppenheimer's embrace of a kind of *shadow trinity* as the very name of his test site. I cannot help but recall the dark places where Christianity, under the influence of empire, has lost its way. When not ignoring Trinity altogether, we've instead debased our telling of this Three-in-One as a command-and-control caricature: distinct from the biblical Trinity or mystical

---

81. See http://www.poetryfoundation.org/poems-and-poets/poems/detail/44106.
82. The Exploratorium in San Francisco. See their reflection "Oppenheimer, the Poems, and Trinity," exploratorium.edu/doctoratomic/2_1R.swf.
83. See Alex Wellerstein, "The First Light of Trinity," *New Yorker* (July 16, 2015), newyorker.com/tech/elements/the-first-light-of-the-trinity-atomic-test.

Trinity, *this* is a hierarchical delegation where a single-minded father-ruler demands that an expediently-dispatched son use immense power (or force) to batter and *break* humanity.

Tragically, this is the vision of God that wins out all too often. And—from abusive relationships to the creation of astonishing weapons of mass destruction—this vision has consequences.

Oppenheimer wasn't blind to these consequences. It seems he feared that in breaking open the atom, they enacted an *undoing* or *reversal* of trinity, destabilizing the tripartite atom and disrupting the source code of reality. It's no wonder that, upon witnessing its awful first blast, he immediately invoked the Hindu deity Vishnu, quoting from the *Bhagavad Gita*, "Now I am become death, the destroyer of worlds."[84]

Our imaginations, applied to worlds "above" and "below," can be used for such potent life *and* death.[85] This is part of the mystery of freedom that God grants us. This particular mystery of exploding power, as atomic scientists have told me, is not found in the protons. It's not found in the electrons, or neutrons either.

Believe it or not, the explosive power is found in the *interaction* between them. It's called nuclear power, and it can change everything.

Does this put the Trinity in perspective for you? We're not talking gobbledygook in trying to describe the Triune mystery, though you can be forgiven if you think it sounds like that, especially in my struggling formulations. Theologians and contemplatives describing the Three-in-One dance are not unlike physicists describing the mystery of atomic energy: they say it's not only stranger than it sounds, it's even stranger than we can normally understand.[86]

---

84. To hear a haunting, ambient musical setting of Oppenheimer's actual statement, look up Linkin Park's "The Radiance" from *A Thousand Suns*, their 2010 album meditating on the nuclear fears that Oppenheimer and his collaborators unleashed.

85. See Proverbs 18:21.

86. The saying "The universe is not only stranger than we think but even stranger than we are capable of thinking" is widely attributed to German theoretical physicist Werner Heisenberg. Similarly, British geneticist, biometrician, and physiologist J. B. S. Haldane said, "Now, my own suspicion is that the universe is not only queerer than we suppose, but queerer than we can suppose." See J. B. S. Haldane, "Possible Worlds," *Possible Worlds and Other Papers*, 1927.

The Perennial Tradition has often said, "As above, so below." (The Perennial Tradition *gathers* traits common in the world's wisdom lineages.) "God in his heaven" directly impacts things "here on earth below." We see echoes of this reciprocal language even in the Lord's Prayer: *"Your kingdom come, your will be done, on earth as it is in heaven."*[87] If we update this language for the quantum era—moving from the "Great Chain of Being" to the "Nested Holarchy of Being," as the philosopher Ken Wilber puts it,[88] we can rightly speak of *As within, so without.* If all reality is a holon and has a fractal character, as physicists are also telling us, then each part contains and mirrors the whole. If the cosmos as we know it originates from a "big bang"—from a "Let there be"—that means that *one point* just *explodes* with life and gives birth to *the many lives.*

When does this *many* cease to be *one?*

When did this *one* ever *not* contain the *many?*

Never! This is what the relational pattern of the universe is teaching us, from Godhead to geochemistry and everything in between.

The shape of the cosmos—quasar to quark—is triune.

How do we practice this presence—of reality? Scientists and mystics alike will tell us: Be present! Experiment! Stay curious. This is Contemplation 101. Let go of what you "think" is your intelligence center—because what you think is your intelligence cannot understand the atom, cannot understand the galaxies, and cannot understand what is birthing and animating all existence.

This momentous truth can occasionally be *caught* but not easily *taught.*

We're standing in the middle of an awesome mystery—life itself!—and the only appropriate response before this mystery is humility. If we're resolved that this is where we want to go—into the mystery, not to hold God and reality but to let God and reality hold us—then I think religion is finally in its proper and appropriate place.

---

87. Matthew 6:10 (NIV).
88. See Ken Wilber, "From the Great Chain of Being to Postmodernism in Three Easy Steps" (2006), 2, 4, www.kenwilber.com/Writings/PDF/FromGC2PM_GENERAL_2005_NN.pdf.

ARISTOTLE AND BOETHIUS: THE PRICE OF AN INVADING NOUN

When we built on Aristotle's belief that substance is a higher and pre-ferred category than relationship (to put it another way, that nouns are better than verbs), we inherited an absolutely non-Trinitarian notion of the human person that was autonomous, static, and without a metaphysi-cal capacity for union with our own beings, much less the divine nature of God.[89] In this metaphysically hamstrung version of reality, we were *not* created in "the image and likeness of God," after all!

We have spent two thousand years of ineffective spirituality trying to overcome this foundational incompatibility between divinity and human-ity, as reflected in everything from dense systematic tomes to awkwardly-intrusive "evangelism" tracts proposing unbridgeable gulfs, their medium *and* message the antithesis of relationship.

Although Jesus broke through and gave us the truth theologically, we have not grounded it theologically. We did not have an underlying philoso-phy (and thus anthropology) to back up relational belonging and mutual participation as anything more than soft sentiment or a pious hope.

Boethius (480–524), whose *Consolations of Philosophy* had great influ-ence throughout the entire medieval period, acted as a sort of bridge between classical Western culture and Christianity. He defined the human being as "an individual substance of a rational nature," and in some ways this definition has persisted to this day. There is no evidence Boethius was influenced by the doctrine of the Trinity, and it shows.

What thus won out in our entire Western anthropology was human *individuality* and human *rationality*, instead of *foundational relationality* and an honoring of the *intuitive* nature of the human person, which is healthy religion's natural habitat. A Trinitarian theology would have told us that human personhood is a *subsistent relation* at its core, generating, in fact, relationships of unconditional love with the same standing as the persons of the Trinity. This is precisely the best description of what we mean when we quote Genesis to say that we are created "in the image and likeness of God." But we did not build on this Trinitarian grounding.

89. Contrast this with 2 Peter 1:4 (NIV), "[God] *has given us his very great and precious promises, so that through them you may participate in the divine nature, having escaped the corruption in the world caused by evil desires.*"

The fallout of privileging "substance" over relationship is difficult to overestimate. The entire subsequent tradition had a very hard time giving any solid, inherent foundation to the meaning of divine union, holiness, salvation, or even incarnation. This is a huge price to pay; the consequence is an eviscerated Christian theology, a hollowed-out shell known for little else than a soft and sentiment-laden worldview.

SCOTUS AND MERTON: TIME TO RE-VERB

In order to be vital, we must be able to demonstrate a metaphysical core for Christian spirituality and holiness—not merely a behavioral, psychological, or moral one. A Trinitarian metaphysic provides just such a vibrant and inherent core. Trinity is and must be our *stable, rooted identity* that does not come and go, rise and fall. This is the rock of salvation.

And of course, it's so interesting that this stable root is rather perfectly mirrored in the three particles of every atom orbiting and cycling around one another—the basic physical building block of the universe. What happens if these atoms are intentionally destabilized? Precisely a bomb of death and destruction.

In many permutations that have led us to modern individualism, most Christians still have retained a more "pagan" understanding of the human person, almost totally reversing the original Trinitarian use of the word *person*—as one who is a dynamic *sounding-through*—to an autonomous self that, at the end of the day, is kin to nothing.

What would it look like to rebuild on a Trinitarian metaphysic and recreate a truly human full personhood?

It would start by recognizing that each person is created by God as unique and irreplaceable—one to whom God has transferred and communicated God's divine image in relationship, and who can, in turn, communicate and reflect that image to other created beings. Each and every one of us. Merton discovered this solid grounding in a Trinitarian and "personalist" philosophy and theology in the work of a thirteenth-century Franciscan philosopher-theologian, John Duns Scotus. A deep-dive into Scotus allowed Merton to move to the heights of contemplative awareness. Most do not get to enjoy this core; salvation and holiness become just a wish, a hope, at best a verbal affirmation that "I and the Father are one." But all too often—in contemporary religion and spirituality alike—we have no basis in consistent, fleshed-out thinking to really believe this.

Thus the vast majority of Christians have not been able to overcome the gap between Divine Personhood and human personhood. It largely became a matter of trying to overcome it by a magical notion of sacraments if you were Catholic or Orthodox, or a transactional notion of "strong belief" or moral behavior if you were Protestant. But in either case, there was no inherent capacity for divine union that could be evoked and built upon in our very soul. Thus, it was consistently a very *unstable* core for most Christians, often degenerated into a kind of make-believe, if we're honest.

THE PERFECT FREEDOM OF GOD

This solid core of a soul, entirely relationally created, is fully known and fully loved only in God—and even *as God*, as daring as this sounds.

To put it concretely, *we are included in the self-knowledge and self-love of God from the very beginning.* Read this stirring, ancient apostolic letter (lightly paraphrased), as if for the first time, and know this is not just my idea:

> Blessed be the God and Father of our Lord Jesus Christ, who has blessed us in Christ with every spiritual blessing in the heavenly places, just as God chose us in Christ before the foundation of the world to be holy and blameless before God in love.

> God destined us for adoption as holy children through Jesus Christ, according to the good pleasure of the divine will, to the praise of the glorious grace that God freely bestowed on us in the Beloved.

> In Christ we have redemption through his blood, the forgiveness of our trespasses, according to the riches of his grace that he lavished on us.

> With all wisdom and insight, God has made known to us the mystery of the divine will, according to God's good pleasure that he set forth in Christ, as a plan for the fullness of time, to gather up all things in Christ, things in heaven and things on earth.

In Christ we have also obtained an inheritance, having been destined according to the purpose of the One who accomplishes all things according to Divine counsel and will, so that we, who were the first to set our hope on Christ, might live for the praise of his glory.

In him you also, when you had heard the word of truth, the gospel of your salvation, and had believed in him, were marked with the seal of the promised Holy Spirit; this is the pledge of our inheritance toward redemption as God's own people, to the praise of Divine glory.[90]

Personhood is not a static notion, but an entirely dynamic and relational one (*per sonare*) that is shared between the divine persons and all human persons—*by reason and gift of their creation*. Not by reason of any later joining, realizations, sacraments, or affirmations, although these are needed and often profoundly help us return to our original identity in God.

All human personhood implies a process of *coming to be* in love!

Sin is every refusal to move in the direction of our deepest identity as love.

Any definition of the person as a substance instead of a relationship tends to leave out the movement, growth, and mutual mirroring that moves us forth in existence.

Selfhood is thus always hidden in a promising darkness, an opaque revelation that we can slowly allow, trust, and lend ourselves to. This is the core of faith.

Based on Scotus's notion of the perfect freedom of God, God initially knows and loves all possible "creatables" (*creabilia*) in Godself—which we Christians would call the Son, the Christ, the *Logos*—the Pattern that holds everything in potential and in essence.

But then, by a free act, God *chooses* some of these to come forth into existence as a *this* (person)!

God freely selects which of the possibilities come into existence, according to Scotus; this is God's most perfect and free act of love, without any compulsion or sin problem to solve.

---

90. Ephesians 1:3–14, based on the *New International Version*.

Thus, just like the Trinity, we are not a *substance*, but a *relationship*.

Always in the process of being loved and passing along love.

God knows and loves us before God wills us, and God's free-willing of us is Trinity's further act of unique subsistent relationship with us. We are loved into being, because love can only exist inside of freedom. This first, perfect, and totally free act of love is that God gratuitously chooses us to exist.

CREATIVE CONTINUATION

Daniel Walsh, who was Merton's primary philosophy teacher, says he's not sure if the human person can even legitimately be called a *creation*, because we are a continuance, an emanation from, a subsistent relation with what we call Trinity.[91] We are in continuity with God somehow, and not a separate creation. We are "chosen in Christ before the foundation of the world," as Ephesians puts it.[92]

Mature Christianity is thus an invitation to share in the personal life of God, a dynamic of generated love forever continued in space and time through God's creatures.

Thus, God's self-knowledge includes knowledge of us, and God's self-love includes love of us.

They are the same knowing, the same loving, and the same freedom.

Yes, in some sense we become an "other" that can be seen as a separate object from God, but from God's side we are always known and loved *subject to subject*, just as the persons of the Trinity know and love one another. God and the human person must know (and can know) one another center to center, subject to subject—and never subject to object.

This is the perhaps the clearest way to describe God's unconditional acceptance of us, forgiveness of our mistakes, and mercy toward us in all circumstances:

We are never an object to God. God cannot but love God's image in us.

---

91. Daniel Walsh, unpublished notes from his teaching at the Gethsemani monastery. Walsh taught regularly at the monastery from the late 1950s to the early 1960s.
92. See Ephesians 1:4.

So a fully Christian theology and philosophy of the human person must say that human personhood originates in the divine Logos, the eternal Christ, as imitations and reflections of God's relationship to Godself. We are constituted by the same relationship that exists between the Father, Son, and Holy Spirit!

"The end for which the human person is created is to manifest the Truth of Christ in the love God has for himself in his Divine Trinity," Daniel Walsh says in his lectures to the monks. This is the theology of personhood upon which Thomas Merton builds his monumental worldview, and which we can, too.

Divine Personhood and human personhood are reciprocal, mutually-mirroring concepts. God's nature as relationship creates ours, and ours is constituted by this same bond, which is infinite openness and capacity to love.

We must know that we are in fact objectively loveable to really be able to love ourselves. That is what Divine Personhood assures and guarantees. Your false self is not ready for unconditional love. Love and respect, yes. But not unconditional love—only conditional love.

This becomes Merton's foundation for what he calls the True Self, which is always, objectively, and forever completely loveable—all ephemera notwithstanding. I believe this was supposed to be the foundational good news of the gospel, the rock of salvation—a basis for human personhood that does not vacillate and cannot fail. Jesus is announcing with his words and exemplifying with his Table and teaching alike that human persons are created inside of the substantial and infinite love of the Trinity. You cannot "get" to such a place; you can only rest and rejoice in such a place.

PARADIGMS LOST

So God is not first of all a "being" that loftily decides to love good people and punish bad people; instead, Absolute Love stands revealed as the very name and shape of Being itself. Love constitutes the very nature of being, as opposed to a seemingly demanding and whimsical being occasionally deciding to love or not to love, which gives the human psyche a very fragile and shaky foundation.

Trinity is the ultimate paradigm shift; it was supposed to come standard-installed in the Christian revelation. Again, it should have changed everything, but it didn't. The doctrine of the Trinity was largely shelved as an embarrassing abstraction—even by most preachers, teachers, and theologians. God was diminished, and we all lost out. Jesus alone was forced to carry the entire drama of liberation, which he could do, it seems; but there was always a much bigger foundation, frame, dynamic, and energy missing from the salvation equation.

Here's how Julian of Norwich experienced this reality, all the way back in fourteenth- and fifteenth-century England:

> The Trinity suddenly filled my heart with the greatest joy. And I understood that in heaven it will be like that for ever for those who come there. For the Trinity is God, God is the Trinity; the Trinity is our maker and protector, the Trinity is our dear friend for ever, our everlasting joy and bliss, through our Lord Jesus Christ. And this was shown in the first revelation, and in all of them; for it seems to me that where Jesus is spoken of, the Holy Trinity is to be understood.[93]

We cannot separate Jesus from the Trinity. Yet the average person in the pews never had a chance to enjoy the much bigger economy of grace. We swam around in a small pool called scarcity, which is now evident in most of our stingy, hoarding politics and economics.

Even our old catechisms said that the "theological virtues" of faith, hope, and love, which were said to be the nature of Divine Being, were offered to us as "a sharing in the very life of God." These, it was argued in the medieval church, were not first of all gifts to individuals but gifts to society, history, and humanity as a whole.[94]

This is prefigured in two great thinkers in the Church, Augustine and Aquinas, who argued that the virtue of hope applies first of all to the collective before the individual.

---

93. Julian of Norwich, *Revelations of Divine Love*, trans. Elizabeth Spearing (New York: Penguin Classics, 1998), 46.
94. See Von Balthasar, *Dare We Hope?*

Yet we tried to generate hope in the isolated individual, while leaving him and her adrift in a cosmos, society, and humanity that was heading toward hopelessness and punishment.

It is very hard for individuals to enjoy faith, hope, and love, or even to *preach* faith, hope, and love—which alone last[95]—unless society itself first enjoys faith, hope, and love in some collective way. This is much of our problem today; we have not given the world any message of cosmic hope, but only threatening messages of Apocalypse and Armageddon.

God as Trinity gives hope to society as a whole, because it is based on the very nature of existence itself and not on the up-and-down behaviors of individuals, which are always unstable. Stay with me here, and I think this problem and its answer will become obvious.

Nevertheless, let's first turn to the example of children to assess this individual virtue of hope, since we have to begin with our own humanity. Marketing experts say children (and dogs) are even more effective than sex in advertising. Why? Because children and dogs are still filled with a natural hope and expectation that their smile will be returned. They tend to make direct eye contact, looking right into you, just grinning away (unless, of course, they have been abused).

This is pure being.

This is uninhibited flow.

Surely, this is why Jesus told us to be like children. There is nothing stopping the pure flow in a child or a dog, and that's why any of us who have an ounce of eros, humanity, or love in us are defenseless against such unguarded presence.

You can only with great effort resist kissing a wide-eyed baby or petting an earnest dog. You want to pull them to yourself with love because they are, for a moment—forgive me—"*God*"!

Or is it the other way around? Is it *you* who have become "God" by standing in such an unresisted flow?

Both are true, of course. We see this flow in the attraction of all beauty, in all admiring, in all ecstasy, in all solidarity with any suffering. Anyone

---

95. See 1 Corinthians 13:13.

who fully allows the flow will see the divine image even in places that have become ugly or undone. This is the universal seeing of the Trinity.

"Anyone who lives in love lives in God, and God lives in him."[96]

If I had said that independently of St. John, many would have called me a lightweight New Ager from California, but I simply share John's deeply Trinitarian spirituality—in all its implications. This is true Traditionalism.

What Trinity is saying, sisters and brothers, is that God, as I expressed earlier, is actually inter-being, which many Buddhists are freer to say than we are. What irony! Yet we know truth is one, so it should not surprise or disappoint us. We were the ones who should have been taught via Trinity that God was not *a* being, surely not an isolated anything—which, of course, implies that all creatures proceeding from such a Source are inter-beings, also.

This shines light on our fascination with sexuality, with all things beautiful, with nature, with animals, with music and art; we are naturally drawn to lovely things outside and beyond ourselves, and we want to rush toward them and unite with them in almost any way—some ways that work and some that frankly don't (which we might call addictive behavior or "sin").

Henceforth, you can know and love God on at least three distinctly wonderful levels: the Transpersonal level ("Father"), the Personal level ("Jesus"), and the Impersonal level ("Holy Spirit"). If you are interested, this rather perfectly corresponds to what Ken Wilber and others call "the One Two Three of God."[97]

Once you look out at reality from inside the Trinity, you can and will know, love, and serve God in all that you do. The metaphors, rituals, and doctrines of other religions are no longer threatening to you, but often very helpful. *God as Trinity makes competitive religious thinking largely a waste of time.* But only mystics seem to know that the only possible language by which we can talk about God is metaphorical.

---

96. 1 John 4:16 (JB).
97. See Ken Wilber, *The One Two Three of God* (Boulder, Colorado: Sounds True, 2006).

DISTINCT UNION

So let's talk more about the Three.

There's a perfect balancing in the Trinity that protects personal identity and total oneness at the same time. We are told that Father, Son, and Holy Spirit (to again use the classic names) each have their uniqueness, and yet they create a deeper and more solid oneness by surrendering it lovingly to one another. (The parallel to authentic sexual encounter is striking.)

And let me say right up front, don't waste too much time trying to argue about the gender of the Three; the male names ascribed to two of them and the common feminine attribution to the Holy Spirit are in great part arbitrary—to the underlying Mystery. What the early theologians overwhelmingly agreed on is that what mattered was *the relationships between them* (a technical term being "the subsistent relations") and not the individual names or genders of the Three. In Scripture, the Creator is referred to as a rock[98] and as a nursing mother;[99] Jesus is referred to as wisdom[100] and as a mother hen;[101] the Holy Spirit is depicted as breath,[102] *ruah* in Hebrew, which is feminine,[103] and is also called *Comforter,* or *Paraclete* in Greek,[104] which is beyond gender altogether.[105] Consider all of these images—as well as others, such as flaming fire[106] and apparently even "wild dog"![107] This is exactly what we'd expect to find in relation to a God in whom male and female are said to reflect something genuine of the divine image and likeness. Clearly, our triune God is a riot of expression, transcending and including any possible labels.

---

98. See, for example, Deuteronomy 32:4; Psalm 18:2.
99. See, for example, Isaiah 49:14–15.
100. See 1 Corinthians 1:30.
101. See, for example, Matthew 23:37.
102. See, for example, John 20:22.
103. See, for example, Psalm 104:29–30.
104. See John 14:26 (KJV). Other translations use *"Helper," "Counselor,"* and *"Advocate."*
105. For a comprehensive—though not exhaustive—look at feminine images for God (Creator, Redeemer, and Spirit) in the Bible, see mikemorrell.org/2012/05/biblical-proofs-for-the-feminine-face-of-God-in-scripture. And for an excellent exploration of nonhuman imagery for God in Scripture, see Lauren Winner's *Wearing God: Clothing, Laughter, Fire, and Other Overlooked Ways of Meeting God* (San Francisco: HarperOne, 2015).
106. See Isaiah 4:5.
107. See B. Doyle, "God as a Dog: Metaphorical Allusions in Psalm 59," in *Metaphor in the Hebrew Bible,* ed. P. Van Hecke (Leuven, Belgium: Leuven University Press, 2005), 41–54.

The all-important thing is that the Three are formed and identified by the outpouring and uninhibited flow itself. The flow forms and protects the Three, and the Three distribute the flow. It's precisely this same dynamic for a healthy society, isn't it?

But we tend to dwell in extremes. In much of the West today, it's either intense individualism (in both its progressive *and* conservative forms)—making the common good a lost and impossible ideal; or people live in mindless collectives, tribalism, and groupthink—where too many people lack any healthy autonomy or personal individuation (again in both progressive and conservative formats, which shows us this common way of seeing offers us two bogus criteria for truth).

So how can we *preserve deep and true values across the spectrum?* This is invariably the question. Honestly, without trying to be esoteric, the Trinity gives us a rather ideal paradigm, model, and invitation. A way through that could be applied to so many problematic and political issues.[108] Let's again try.

The word *person* as we use it today, meaning a separate human individual, is not really found in the Hebrew Bible. But the idea of "face" is. Hebrew authors wanted to convey the effect of "interface" with their YHWH God who sought to intimately communicate with them: "May God let his face shine upon you, and may his face give you peace."[109] This same usage is found in several psalms,[110] where it is often translated as *presence*, meaning more precisely *communicated presence*—a transference of selfhood from one to another.

In the Greek translations of the Bible that we have, the noun used for "face" was *prosopon*, literally referring to the stage masks that Greek actors wore. This seemed to serve as both an enlarged identity and a megaphone. Teachers like Tertullian and the Cappadocian Fathers used similar language, in Latin *persona*, preserving the full freedom and identity of what

---

108. Dave Andrews, an Australian teacher, theologian, activist, and community organizer, has written an invaluable community formation resource based on a deep understanding of Trinitarian relationship. It's difficult to find in North America, but see his Compassionate Community Work Course at www.daveandrews.com.au/ccwc.html.
109. See Numbers 6:25–26.
110. See Psalm 42:2; 89:15–16; 95:2.

were eventually called the three "persons" of the Trinity—who are nevertheless a perfect and total communion.

Each member of the Trinity was considered a *persona*, or "face," of God. Each person of the Trinity fully communicated its face and goodness to the other, while fully maintaining its own *facial identity* within itself. Each person of the Trinity "sounded through" (*per sonare*) the other.

Ironically, *person* is now our word for the autonomous human being, but originally it meant almost exactly the opposite. Each of the Three knew they were *soundings-through* from the other two. Identity was both maintained and fully shared, which frankly is what makes any mature love possible. Every good psychologist would agree.

We are each a sounding-through of something much more and even of Someone Else, and that becomes our *self*. Yet we are a stage mask, a face, receiving and also revealing our shared DNA, our ancestors, and our past culture. This has formed our very understanding of what we now call a "person." Again, ironically, what first implied that all identity was shared now means the exact opposite—a separate individual is now called a "person," and we do not commonly honor the fact that we are all "soundings-through"! This simple distortion has made the first Catholic moral principle of "the common good" almost an impossible ideal.

Think of your own experience: how many people do you know, including yourself, who are really in this divine dance with an appropriate and balanced degree of self-love and self-giving? It is the very definition of psychological maturity. And it is indeed a dance, where we all make a lot of missteps.

Insofar as an appropriate degree of self-love is received, held, enjoyed, trusted, and participated in, this is the same degree to which it can be given away to the rest of the world. You can and you must "love your neighbor *as you love yourself*"—for your own wholeness and theirs.

The Golden Rule is also the gold standard for all growth and development. We learned it from the Trinity.

This is the never-ending dance: the movement in and out, of receiving and handing on.

And remember, if it's not flowing out of you, it's probably because you're not allowing it to flow toward you. And love can flow toward you in every moment: through the image in a flower, in a grain of sand, in a wisp of cloud, in any one person whom you allow to delight you. It's why you begin to find yourself smiling at things for no apparent reason.

TIDE BOXES AT KMART

One time, I was in the detergent aisle at my local Kmart in Albuquerque. I know, this story is starting out promising, right? Stay with me!

I was the only one in that aisle—thankfully—and I found myself just standing there, smiling at the Tide boxes.

I'm not sure how long I was doing this, but it was a solid few minutes, I suspect. Eventually, I recovered and looked both ways, grateful that no one was watching, because I was a little embarrassed by my silly smile. Such causeless grinners are usually unstable people, aren't they? I knew that, normally, *Tide boxes* are not great causes of joy in and of themselves.

Or are they? Should Proctor and Gamble hire me?

Spiritual joy has nothing to do with anything "going right." It has everything to do with things *going*, and *going on* within you. It's an inherent, inner aliveness. Joy is almost entirely an inside job. Joy is not first determined by the object enjoyed as much as by the prepared eye of the enjoyer.

And when the flow is flowing, it doesn't matter what you're doing. You don't have to be a priest on the altar or a preacher in a pulpit, that's for sure. (I can hear the palpable relief all the way over here from this keyboard. You're welcome.)

You can be a homemaker in a grocery store or a construction worker at a work site; it doesn't matter. It's *all* inherently sacred and deeply satisfying. As the nineteenth-century poet Elizabeth Barrett Browning put it, "Earth's crammed with heaven, and every common bush afire with God."[111]

All is whole and holy in the very seeing, because you are standing inside the One Flow of Love without the negative pushback of *doubting*.[112]

---

111. From *Aurora Leigh*; read it in its entirety at http://www.bartleby.com/236/86.html.
112. Note Jesus' words to Thomas the doubter in John 20:24–29.

This is all that there really is. Call it Consciousness, call it God, call it Love; this is the Ground of all Being out of which all things—and especially all good things—come.[113]

It's an allowing; it's a deep seeing; it's an enjoying. It is the Creative Force of the universe. The river is already flowing, and you are in it whether you are enjoying it or not.

So what is your "flow" right now?

Are you sucking in or flowing out?

Are you defending or opening up?

Is it negative energy or life energy that controls this day?

Are you over-defensive, or can you be vulnerable before the next moment?

These are two utterly different directions and energies, and you must learn to tell the difference within yourself. Otherwise, you will not know what to pray for, what you actually need, and who you really are in any one moment.[114]

All of your raw material for right-seeing is within you—because in the Holy Spirit you have your inner "Advocate" and "Defense Attorney."[115] The Spirit is your implanted placeholder who teaches you how to pray, how to hope, and how to love. As Paul so honestly says, *"We do not know how to pray."*[116]

You just have to let go of whatever it is within you that is saying no to the flow, judging it as impossible, or of any shame that is keeping the Indwelling Spirit from guiding you, because guess what? Even your sins often become your best teachers. The Great Flow makes use of everything, absolutely everything. Even your mistakes will be used in your favor, if you allow them to be. That's how good God is.

---

113. See James 1:17.
114. Reflect on James 1:19–24. This oldest of New Testament letters sounds almost Buddhist at times in its emphasis on praxis over theory. (Luther, quite unfortunately, did not like James one bit.)
115. See John 14.
116. See Romans 8:26 (JB).

LOVING ALL THE WRONG PEOPLE

"Only *we* have the Spirit."

I was taught this in my church growing up; and then I found that every religion says the same thing. Isn't that interesting?

There's a phrase for this; it's called *group narcissism*. It has nothing to do with love for God; it isn't a search for truth or love. It's a grasping for control, and *every* group at its less mature stages of development will try to put God into the pocket of its own members-only jackets!

Why do I say something so unequivocal? Because I dare you to find a world religion that doesn't do this. But we don't need to look any further than our own Old Testament. Here are some prevalent religious mind-sets from those times that were carried over into Jesus' first-century world—and how Jesus responds to them.

"God ignores the Samaritans."

The Samaritans, living in proximity to the Jewish people, were considered a mixed race with "mixed" religion, and were therefore not to be associated with, as John's gospel explains matter-of-factly: *"Jews, of course, do not associate with Samaritans"* (John 4:9). But then Jesus tells a parable praising the extraordinary kindness of a Samaritan (see Luke 10:25–37); another time, when he travels through Samaria, he surprises a Samaritan woman—as well as his own disciples—by talking to her directly, engaging her in a conversation about deep spiritual matters. (See John 4:4–42.) Jesus also displays God's favor toward Samaritans in other ways. (See, for example, Luke 9:52–56; 17:11–19.)

"God does not know that the Syrophoenicians even exist."

The Syrophoenicians, living north of Israel, were considered outsiders and pagans. But a Syrophoenician woman, desperate for her daughter to be healed, appeals to Jesus, who praises her for her great faith and heals her daughter. (See Mark 7:24–30; Matthew 15:22–28.)

"We are the chosen people—to the exclusion of all other peoples."

While affirming God's unique relationship with Israel, Jesus demonstrates God's grace toward and inclusion of people of all backgrounds—something his disciples and the crowds didn't expect. When Jesus' disciples finally came to understand his purpose, they did the same. They saw that all peoples—whether Jews, Jewish proselytes, or other "Gentiles" or "foreigners"—could enter the circle dance of the Trinity and experience the Spirit poured out upon them. (See, for example, Acts 2:1–11; 10:1–49.)

Jesus messes everything up! What does he do? He consistently makes the outsider the heroes of his parables and the recipients of God's multifaceted grace. To not recognize and learn from this is culpable ignorance at this point.

By and large, we didn't get it. Catholicism replicated almost down to fine detail the ritual and legalistic mistakes of Judaism, and Protestantism has imitated us quite well, while trying to cover their tracks by just getting legalistic about very different issues. But it is the same ego game.

And one could easily argue that our fellow Abrahamic path, Islam, has followed suit in mirroring our most egregious members-only behavior. Because that's where immature religion always finds itself; it isn't first of all a search for Holy Mystery and how to love. Most early religion is a search for the egoic self, a search for the moral high ground, and certainly for being better than those *other* people over there.

To draw from Karl Rahner again, he suggested that for fifty years we should all basically stop using the word *God*. Because, he says, we normally don't have a clue what we are talking about! This becomes quite evident when we see what we have done with Jesus himself, who was given as the fully *visible and obvious* manifestation—and we still used him for our small culture wars. We still pulled him inside of our smaller psyche and out of the protective silence of the Trinity. We pretended we understood him perfectly whenever we could interpret him for our own wars, prejudices, and dominations. Poor Jesus.

So let's just be humble and call God "the Holy Mystery" for fifty years, to cauterize the wound we've inflicted on our culture and ourselves. And maybe, as Rahner suggested, after half a century, we can get the language clarified and a little more humble, deferring to this Holy Mystery in grateful recognition that we're not in charge of very much and we understand very little.

EMPTINESS ALONE IS PREPARED FOR FULLNESS

To make the above subhead real, let me quote from one of the earliest hymns of the church:

His state was divine
yet he did not cling
to his equality with God
but emptied himself.[117]

Could this first stanza of the great Philippian hymn, in its fullness, be applied not only to Jesus but also perhaps to the entire Trinity? I believe so.

The Three all live as an eternal and generous self-emptying, the Greek word being *kenosis*.

If you're protecting yourself, if you're securing your own image and identity, then you're still holding on. Your ego remains full of itself. The opposite of *kenosis*.

The intriguing thing about the mutuality of the Trinity is that the names—the roles—the energies—are really interchangeable.

We don't want to typecast the Father as the only infinite one, the Son as the only imminent one, or the Spirit as the only intimate one! All is absolutely given to the other and let go of; but for the sake of our mind, it's helpful to identify three persons.

When all three of those divine qualities start drawing you, and when you're at home with Infinity, Imminence, and Intimacy—all Three—I think you're finally living inside a full Trinitarian spirituality.

This is God's lifetime, lifelong work in you.

I hope this does not surprise or disappoint you, but I have often noticed these divine qualities in people who are marginalized, oppressed, "poor," or "mentally disabled"—more than in many others.

They have to trust love. They need communion. They know that only the vulnerable people understand them. They profit from mutuality. They're always in relationship. They find little ways to serve their community, to

---

117. Philippians 2:6 (JB).

serve the sick, to serve those poorer than themselves. They know that *only a suffering God can save them.*

You can take such a pattern as the infallible sign that one lives in God. People filled with the flow will always move away from any need to protect their own power and will be drawn to the powerless, the edge, the bottom, the plain, and the simple. They have all the power they need—and it always overflows, and like water seeks the lowest crevices to fill.

THE SPACE BETWEEN

Sometimes, people try to over-define the Trinity. "*This* is the work of the Father," they say, confidently. "*This* is the role of the Son. And *this* is what the Spirit looks like." In attempting to parse out and diagram the persons of Trinity, something vital is lost: the space between them.

The inner life of Godhead—this is a mystery that stretches language to its breaking point. The specific functions or roles of each person can be interesting to ponder, but frankly I don't think this is the important point. Even the three names are largely "placeholders," and a thousand beautiful names for God can be interchanged with each of them, as I do with names for the Holy Spirit in the appendix to this book, and as we have always done with both Christ and Jesus.

The all-important thing is to get the *energy* and *quality* of the relationship between these Three—that's the essential mystery that transforms us.

Finally, it's something you can experience only by resting inside of the relationships (prayer?), as when the disciples asked Jesus where he lived, and he offered this intimate invite: "*Come and see.*"[118] Divine hospitality at work.

For years, the metaphor I've used for this is something most parents can readily relate to. When your little ones are getting ready to sleep, you can make the most comfortable bed and bassinette for them that you want, but will they stay there? No! Every excuse they can, they're going to crawl in bed between the two of you, aren't they?

---

118. John 1:39.

And I'm sure you love it. Maybe not *every* night, but at least sometimes, before they start digging their heels into your neck!

Why do children like to crawl in your bed like this?

Because that's where all the energy is!

All the safety and tenderness that they want!

Between the two of you.

They've got the best of both of you; they literally rest in the space, the relationship, between you. What child wouldn't want to snuggle in bed sleeping between mom and dad?

It must be nirvana! It must be heaven! It must be total security; they can just reach out throughout the night and feel both of you on each side. Whereas each parent represents a certain kind of energy that might otherwise be entrenched on its own, the introduction of a third—the child—adds something truly novel to the mix. Some spiritual students call this "the Law of Three" and say it's how *all* true change takes place.

HOW THE LAW OF THREE CHANGES EVERYTHING

Think about it: It's election season, and you feel passionate about your favorite political candidate. You represent "first force" in the Law of Three—you're in your candidate's corner. Your co-worker—or maybe your parent—backs the *other* candidate of the *other* political party with equal passion. They represent "second force."

The way we live so much of our lives stops right there. Someone takes position A, and someone else opposes them in Position B; they exist in rivalry and antagonism, world without end. This is precisely the behavior we'd expect in a binary system—a place of "two-ness" in opposition. At best, when we're finished yelling at each other, we might try to compromise and form some kind of "synthesis" position out of our dialectic. This is how the philosopher Hegel saw the world: one of dueling dualisms.

But the Law of Three asks the question we've been asking: What if we don't live in a *binary* universe, but instead a *ternary* universe?

If three-ness captures the essence of the cosmos more than two-ness, it means that we can hold our first-force or second-force perspectives with earnestness, while fully awaiting some *third* force to arrive and surprise us all out of our neat little boxes. Note that this isn't some mere synthesis of you and your co-worker's opposition, but something genuinely *novel* arriving on the scene, a Position C.

It could be a viable third-party candidate that captures imaginations; it could be an upset within one of *your* political parties. It might be something on the outside that's "bad," like a storm or a natural disaster, which brings your community together in an unprecedented way. It could be an entirely non-"political" solution that presents itself with such urgency and vitality that everyone forgets—even if for only a season—what they were arguing about.

The exact form third force takes is beside the point, nor is it that first and second force suddenly find themselves invalidated in the face of some newer, shinier debut. Instead, it's that this third force redeems *each* position and gives *everyone* a valuable role to play in the creation of something genuinely new—a fourth possibility that becomes the *new* field of our collective arising.

As I once spent an entire book offering to anyone with ears to hear, *everything belongs*.

This is what we can expect to not just believe as an idea, but experience in practice. If we embrace the life of Trinity at work in all creation, we sit invited at Rublev's lovely round table:

The magic of three breaks us out of our dualistic impasses, and always invites a fourth world for us to enter into.[119]

---

119. Cynthia Bourgeault, my friend, colleague, and co-teacher in the Living School, has penned an excellent book exploring these themes, called *The Holy Trinity and the Law of Three: Discovering the Radical Truth at the Heart of Christianity* (Boston: Shambhala, 2013), which I have cited previously. This book—an exploration of the doctrine of the Trinity paired with the teachings of an enigmatic, turn-of-the-twentieth-century, Turkish-Russian teacher, G. I. Gurdjieff—is so unique in its own right that my brief Law of Three example will have to suffice here. That said, I highly recommend you check her book out in its entirety if you're feeling called to further explore the Trinitarian implications of the Law of Three. And if you're interested in our Living School offerings, go to https://cac.org/living-school.

IS THE TRINITY A BOY OR A GIRL?

"Father" and "Son" are obviously very masculine names for members of the Trinity, and even "Holy Spirit" is often envisioned in masculine terms. As the past two hundred years has led to a recovery of the full dignity and worth of women, both in the culture at large and in the church, many wonder why our language about God is so masculine-heavy.

Here's how I've attempted to resolve this in my own inner devotional life: I have accepted that thousands of years of agrarian, Paleolithic, Fertile Crescent, patriarchal, and finally imperial inertia influenced the appearance of largely masculine names for God.[120]

But you know what I believe? I think the spaces in between the members of the Trinity are unmistakably feminine. The forms or manifestations strike me as the masculine dimension, and the diffused, intuitive, mysterious, and wonderful unconscious in-between, that's the feminine. And *that's* where the essential power is—the space between the persons more than the persons individually.

That said, I think we've done a very good thing in recent years giving the feminine nature of God her due in our biblical studies, our theology, and our worship. Our witness to the divine feminine in worship is particularly important, so people don't come away with a picture of God as irreducibly masculine.[121]

But precisely what this mystery of Trinity does for me is give me a way to be true to both of these witnesses to the feminine in God. It's okay if you want to keep the persons of God in their traditional masculine language— you don't have to, but it works as long as you start unpackaging, proclaiming, teaching, and understanding the spaces in between, the relationships, the movement of the dance itself between the three persons, which for me is the underlying feminine dimension of God.

This is where the generativity seems to happen—where Hildegard's *veriditas*, or new life, seems to happen. As the scientific principle of William

---

120. To read a fascinating account of how the development of language out of farming practices influenced our naming of God, see Leonard Shlain's *The Alphabet Versus the Goddess: The Conflict Between Word and Image* (New York: Penguin Books, 1999).
121. For a listing of over a hundred feminine images of God in Scripture with references, see http://mikemorrell.org/2012/05/biblical-proofs-for-the-feminine-face-of-God-in-scripture.

of Ockham's "Razor" suggests (one of our lesser-known Franciscan luminaries), the truest answer will usually be both simple and elegant; I find simplicity and elegance in this explanation. So take it into your prayer; walk inside of this masculine/feminine polarity and dance and see if you're not renewed. History up to now has very seldom found the lovely balance.

THE POWER OF CONCENTRIC CIRCLES

What if we actually dropped into this flow and let it be our major teacher? Even our very notion of society, politics, and authority would utterly change, because most of it is still top down and outside in.

It's no surprise that the Western political notion of the divine right of kings held for so many centuries. We still observe that most people are utterly fascinated by other people they think are "important" or "powerful," whether athletes, politicians, spiritual leaders, or celebrities. It is as if they have *mana*, a unique power or energy flowing from "out there" or "up there"—instead of *in here*. Most people live in fascination of and deep codependency on their own form of cargo cult. The power is always out there and up there. I don't think we would operate in this out-of-body way if we were in vital connection with the Trinity and the indwelling Spirit.

Trinitarian theology says that true power is circular or spiral, not so much hierarchical.

It's here; it's within us. It's shared and shareable; it's already entirely for you (see Romans 5:5 and all over the place!). God's Spirit is planted within you and operating *as* you! Don't keep looking to the top of the pyramid. Stop idolizing the so-called "1 percent." There's nothing worthwhile up there that is not also down here. Worst of all, it has given 99 percent of the world an unnecessary and tragic inferiority complex.

Trinity says that God's power is not domination, threat, or coercion, but instead is of a totally different nature, one that even Jesus' followers have not yet adjusted to. If the Father does not dominate the Son, and the Son does not dominate the Holy Spirit, and the Spirit does not dominate the Father or the Son, then there's *no domination in God. All divine power is shared power, which should have entirely changed Christian politics and relationships.*

There's no seeking of *power over* in the Trinity, but only *power with*—a giving away, a sharing, a letting go, and thus an infinity of trust and mutuality. This has the power to change all relationships: in marriage, in culture, and even in international relations. YHWH already tried to teach such servanthood to Israel in the four "servant songs" in order to train them in being "light to all nations,"[122] but their history predicted what Christianity repeated: we both preferred kings and empires instead of any suffering servanthood.

Power, according to the Jesus of the Trinity, is not something to be "grasped at."[123] I, Richard, don't need to cling to my title, my uniform, my authorship, or whatever other trappings I use to make myself feel powerful and important. Waking up inside the Trinitarian dance, I realize that all of this is rather unimportant, in fact often pretense and show that keep me from my True Self. It just gets in the way of honesty and vulnerability and community. We all already have our power (*dynamis*) within us and between us—in fact, Jesus assures us that we are "*clothed*" in it![124]

It seems to me that the only people who can handle power are those who don't need it too much, those who can equally let go of it and share it. In fact, I'd say that at this difficult moment in history, the only people who can handle power are those who have made journeys through *powerlessness*. Most others seem to abuse it, according to the received wisdom of universally practiced male initiation rites.[125]

"Uninitiated" males who too easily acquire power invariably use it for their own purposes of advancement, and seldom for the common good. This hardly needs proof anymore—only love can handle power well. Trinity, the primal and ultimate Sourcer, begins creation by releasing that which empowers everything else: "*Let there be light*"![126]

Light is not really *what* you see; it is *that by which you see* everything else. God is the Great Empowerer, taking the forms of inherent grace and constant evolution. Trinity is so humble that it does not seem to care who

---

122. See Isaiah 42:1–9; 49:1–13; 50:4–9; 52:13–53:12.
123. See the great *kenotic* hymn of Philippians 2:6–7.
124. See Luke 24:49.
125. See Richard Rohr, *Adam's Return* (Chestnut Ridge, NY: Crossroad Publishing Company, 2004).
126. Genesis 1:3.

gets the credit. Like light, you do not see God; but God allows you to see everything else through really good eyes.

This power isn't solitary, either, but shared—reflecting Trinity. As Croatian theologian Miroslav Volf names it:

> Because the Christian God is not a lonely God, but rather a communion of three persons, faith leads human beings into the divine communion. One cannot, however, have a self-enclosed communion with the triune God—a "foursome," as it were—for the Christian God is not a private deity. Communion with this God is at once also communion with those others who have entrusted themselves in faith to the same God. Hence one and the same act of faith places a person into a new relationship both with God and with all others who stand in communion with God.[127]

You've got to know, however, that shared initiation is not the language of corporate America or of most cultures. This is not the language of the 1 percent, who so often "train" us in how to be and what we ought to want. We have to be taught this deeper wisdom right now, or civilization will continue in its rapid downward spiral. Surrender, yielding, trusting, and giving are never going to appeal to the ego. Yet we ignore such embedded wisdom at our impending peril.

The life of faith is not at all "believing impossible things to be true"; actually, it is a much more vigilant path of learning how to rest in an Ultimate Love and how to rest in an Infinite Source. On a very practical level, you will then be able to trust that you are being *held and guided*.

In fact, you can trust after awhile that almost everything is a kind of guidance—absolutely everything.

It's actually your ability to trust that there is guidance available that allows it to show up as guidance! Amazing circular logic, I know, but don't dismiss it until you've sincerely tried it. I'm confident you'll come to see it is true in the divine economy of things.

---

127. Miroslav Volf, *After Our Likeness: The Church as the Image of the Trinity* (Grand Rapids, MI: Eerdmans Publishing Co., 1997), 173.

I warn you, though, that when your calculating mind moves into place, you'll hear yourself appraising these profound moments of judgment: *Oh, that's just a coincidence. That's merely an accident. It just happened.* Or, *Blast, why did that happen?* Or even, *I wish I could change it.* Inside the Trinitarian life, you will begin to enjoy what some physicists now call "quantum entanglement" and what others call synchronicity, coincidence, or accident.

When you doubt even the possibility of such things, you've just stopped the flow! But if you stay on this path of allowing and trusting, the Spirit in you will allow you to confidently surrender: *There's a reason for this. I'm living as the River flows, carried by the surprise of its/my unfolding. I am being led. Cool it. It's okay!*

Please don't hear me as adopting a fatalistic approach, as though you can't work to change or improve your situation. In fact it's quite the contrary—you can. But I *am* saying that what first comes to your heart and soul must be *a yes and not a no, trust instead of resistance.* And when you can lead with your yeses, and allow yourself to see God in all moments, you'll recognize that such energy is never wasted but *always* generates life and light. The saints often called this trust in Divine Providence.

RICHARD OF ST. VICTOR AND THE JOY SUPREME

I discovered that our Franciscan St. Bonaventure (1221–1274), who wrote a lot about the Trinity, was highly influenced by a lesser-known figure called Richard of St. Victor (d. 1173). St. Victor was a very influential monastery in Paris in the early medieval period; so many movers and shakers came from this one monastery that they were collectively called "the Victorines." Many peers kept telling me, *"Richard, read Richard!"* And so I eventually did. And I'm so glad I did! Here is a short summary of what he develops over two chapters much more beautifully:

For God to be good, God can be one. For God to be loving, God has to be two. Because love is always a relationship, right? But for God to "share excellent joy" and "delight"—and this is where his real breakthrough is— God has to be three, because supreme happiness is when two persons share their common delight in a third something—together.[128] All you need to

128. See *Richard of St. Victor: The Book of the Patriarchs, The Mystical Ark, Book Three of the Trinity* (Classics of Western Spirituality) (Mahwah, NJ: Paulist Press, 1979), 387–389.

do is witness a couple at the birth of their new baby, and you know this is supremely true.

When I first read Richard of St. Victor, I remembered what I used to say to people when I first started becoming better known from teaching, speaking, writing, and retreat work. There were a lot of people wanting to get close to me all of a sudden, wanting to be my best friend and so forth. How was I supposed to choose between all these new, would-be friends?

I realized that the people I really loved with great abandon and freedom were not the people who just loved me, but people who loved what I loved. People who cared about community, the gospel, the poor, justice, honesty—this is where the flow was easy, natural, and life-giving. But many other people, it seemed, loved me for all the wrong reasons, needed love more than gifted love, were codependent more than offered creative relationship.

Two people excited about the same thing are the beginning of almost everything new, creative, and risky in our world. Surely this is what Jesus meant by his first and most basic definition of church as "two or three gathered."[129]

So as we've said, we're moving from a binary map of reality into a *ternary* map—reality reflecting a pattern of law and a pattern of three.[130]

I think every one of us has a certain resistance to a ternary map because our whole lives have been formed by binary oppositions. We think in that way. In my book *The Naked Now*, I call it the "dualistic mind." Most people fight back and forth between either/or binaries—just look at our political parties. The one with the loudest voice appears to win, but then you always go away dissatisfied, feeling you have been cheated. And you have been.

At the Center for Action and Contemplation, we try to practice what we call Third Way approaches to conflict, problem-solving, and creativity. You almost have to let "the two" fail you. You almost have to die to them. You almost have to be willing to be disappointed in both of them.

But what most people do—I think to reassure their egos and their need to be right—is to take a stand mightily on one side and make a god out of

---

129. See Matthew 18:20 (NIV, NKJV, KJV).
130. See Bourgeault, *The Holy Trinity and the Law of Three*.

their ideology, religion, or partial truth. But this comes at such a cost! It's such a defeat for intelligence, for wisdom, for depth, for truth.

Stridently taking *sides* in a binary system has nothing to do with truth. The gospel itself is neither liberal nor conservative but severely critiques both sides of this false choice. The true good news of Jesus will never fill stadiums, because dualistic masses can never collectively embrace an enlightened "Third Way," which, contemplatively speaking, always feels a bit like nothing, because in this position you are indeed like Jesus—you have "no place to lay your head."[131]

Just like the mystery of the Father.

Just like the crucifixion of the Son.

Just like the anonymity of the Spirit.

There are commonly two kinds of human beings: there are people who want certitude and there are people who want understanding; and these two cannot understand one another! Really.

Those who demand certitude out of life will insist on it even if it doesn't fit the facts. Logic has nothing to do with it. Truth has nothing to do with it. "Don't bother me with the truth—I've already come to my conclusion!" If you need certitude, you will come to your conclusion. You will surround yourself with your conclusion.

The very meaning of faith stands in stark contrast to this mind-set. Do you know why I think Jesus (or any of the Three) is actually dangerous if taken outside of the Trinity? It's because we then ill-define faith as a very static concept instead of a dynamic and flowing one.

We've turned faith into a right to certitude when, in fact, this Trinitarian mystery is whispering quite the opposite: we have to live in exquisite, terrible humility before reality. In this space, God gives us a spirit of questing, a desire for understanding; it seems to me it's only this ongoing search for understanding that will create compassionate people—and wise people.

If you think you have a right to certitude, then show me where the gospel ever promised you that or offered you that. The New Testament itself is written in a language Jesus never spoke. If God wanted us to

---

131. See Luke 9:58.

have evidence, rational proof, and perfect clarity, the incarnation of Jesus would have been delayed till the invention of audio recorders and video cameras.

Rational certitude is exactly what the Scriptures do *not* offer us. They offer us something much better and an entirely different way of knowing: an intimate relationship, a dark journey, a path where we must discover for ourselves that grace, love, mercy, and forgiveness are absolutely necessary for survival—in an always and forever uncertain world. You only need enough clarity and ground to know how to live without certitude! Yes, we really are saved by *faith*. People who live in this way never stop growing, are not easily defeated, and are frankly fun to live with.

Dave Andrews, an Australian teacher, theologian, activist, and community organizer, puts a contemporary and communal twist on Richard of St. Victor's illuminating maxim:

> It takes *one* person to be an individual. It takes *two* people to make a couple. And it takes at least *three* people to make a community. I like to use the English word "trey," derived from the French word "trei" meaning "three," as a simple, short memorable word for the "threesome"...that creates an exponential explosion in potential—not only in the quantity, but also the quality—of relationships. A trey creates the possibility for people to go beyond personal interest. It is, they say, the beginning of a sense of common cause—a collective purpose—beyond what suits individual interests. A trey creates the *stability* and *security* that is essential for community....
>
> Because the ultimate reality of the universe, depicted in the Trinity, is a community of persons in relation to one another, we know the trey is the only way it is possible for people to relate to one another with the *individuality* of one, the *reciprocity* of two, and the *stability, subjectivity* and *objectivity* of three."[132]

---

132. Dave Andrews, *A Divine Society: The Trinity, Community, and Society* (Eugene, OR: Wipf and Stock Publishers, 2012), 18–19. Emphasis is in the original. Previously published in 2008 by Frank Communications of Queensland, Australia.

THE PARADOX OF RESTLESSNESS AND CONTENTMENT

The authentic Christian life and living inside the flow of Trinity are the same thing—and this flow will always be characterized by two seemingly contradictory things. First, you're going to be constantly yearning and longing for more, the way the Three endlessly desire to give themselves and flow outward. It's a kind of sacred discontent, a holy dissatisfaction, and a holy desire for more life, love, and generativity.

This does *not* arrive, however, out of a sense of emptiness or scarcity, but precisely because you have touched upon *deep contentment* and *abundance*. There's always still more I can do, more I can include and experience; there are more people I can serve. There is more that God wants to give me, and more God wants to ask of me. Any of these will show themselves at different times in the life of a mature Christian. Never "I am fully there, and I have it all." A person who is smug is not inside the Trinitarian flow. How can fullness and still yearning for more so beautifully coexist? I have no answer to that, but I know it to be true.

In the life of the Trinity, you can always rest inside a certain kind of deep contentment: it's all foundationally good and okay. This moment is as perfect as it can be, and I do not need to state my preferences moment by moment, make my judgments or demands, or write my commentary on everything. The judging mind keeps me split and divided from union. This is surely what Paul is referring to when he says of the Christ that "*his nature is all Yes.*"[133] This is the peace the world cannot give nor take away.[134] If a person is not fundamentally resting in the Eternal Sabbath, they are not yet living inside the Trinitarian flow.

There's good news here: all emotional snags, temptations, and mental disruptions are *the negative capability* for this very peace; they invite you to choose again, and each time, you increase your freedom. Trust me on that.

A Trinitarian life is able, therefore, to hold a beautiful kind of creative tension in this world: not afraid to be dependent, while also not afraid to be self-sufficient; able to be self and able to be other—all modeled in the standing lesson of the Trinity. Returning to our thirteenth-century Franciscan

---

133. 2 Corinthians 1:20.
134. See John 14:27; 16:33.

philosopher-theologian John Duns Scotus, he called this *the harmony of goodness*: true love for the self always overflows into love for the other; it is one and the same flow. And your freedom to extend love to others always gives you a sense of dignity and power of your own self. It is such a paradox.

In fact, you cannot have one without the other. Trying to love others without a foundational reverence for yourself ends up as neediness, manipulation, and unsustainable infatuation, expressing itself in endless battles of codependency. Trying to love yourself and not to love others is what we mean by narcissism; this is most dangerous when it takes the form of religious narcissism, which uses even God for its own self-aggrandizement.[135]

You cannot know things if you don't first of all grant them a foundational respect, if you don't love them before you grab them with your mind. This is surely what Genesis warns us against from the beginning, in archetypal Eden:[136] you'll eat voraciously from that forbidden tree of knowledge before you know how to respect and honor what you are eating, which creates very entitled and proud people. All of life becomes a commodity for our consumption.

Paul summarizes this pattern well: "Knowledge puffs up, whereas love builds up. Some may think they have full knowledge of something yet not know it as they ought to know things."[137] Godly knowing is a humble and non-grasping kind of knowledge; it becomes a beautiful process of communion instead of ammunition and power over. It is basically *reverence*! Knowing without loving is frankly dangerous for the soul and for society. You'll critique most everything you encounter and even have the hubris to call this mode of reflexive cynicism "thinking" (whereas it's really your ego's narcissistic reaction to the moment). You'll position things too quickly as inferior or superior, "with me" or "against me," and most of the time you'll be wrong.

To eat of the tree that promises to give you divine knowledge of good and evil is the tree of death.[138] All human knowing is "imperfect" and "[seen] *through a glass, darkly*,"[139] and must necessarily be held with humility and patience.

---

135. See 1 John 2:9–11.
136. See Genesis 2:17.
137. See 1 Corinthians 8:1–2.
138. See Genesis 2:17.
139. 1 Corinthians 13:12 (KJV).

Yet God takes the freedom and immense risk of allowing us to *"eat of all the trees in the garden."*[140] We are even allowed to *"pick from the tree of life too, and eat and live for ever."*[141] The only ones who "must not be allowed to eat" of this tree are precisely those who arrogantly think they are *"like one of us in knowing good from evil."*[142] This is the basic human hubris. An amazing insight! The Genesis text seems to know that such arrogant human knowing will never lead to life for humans, but only death. (Don't let anyone tell you that the creation accounts in Genesis are not profoundly inspired. Note that YHWH again uses the plural in referring to Godself (*"one of us"*), which is quite amazing in a monotheistic religion.

We live in a world where naked knowledge of facts is allowed to have all the sway and all the say. We have many knowledgeable people with doctoral degrees, and technocrats with huge amounts of information. But we have such precious little ability to use this knowledge surplus for the good of the world, or anything really but private superiority. They're probably not bad people at all; but what they might lack is the awareness that all being, modeled on the Trinity, is "good, true, and beautiful" (in Scholastic philosophy, these are called the "three transcendental qualities of being"), and therefore always loveable on some level.

This was John Duns Scotus's doctrine of *"the univocity of being,"* which became the continuing Franciscan opinion.[143] We can speak of all levels of being with "one voice"—from plants, to animals, to humans, to God. I hope you recognize what a breakthrough that is for all poets, mystics, and seers: all is entirely lovable even before it is fully knowable. (The opposite "Dominican" opinion taught that things must be known as true before they can be loved.)

BODY-BASED KNOWING

We are called to embody the love of God in our lives. Not just talk about it or think about it or pray about it. We must live it in our guts, our muscles, our hearts, our eyes, our ears, and our tongues.

---

140. Genesis 2:16.
141. Genesis 3:22.
142. Genesis 3:22.
143. See Rohr, *Eager to Love*, chapter 13, "John Duns Scotus: Anything but a Dunce."

We manifest that love when we share the ordinary rhythm of life with others who are likewise seeking to grow in love and compassion. Such love naturally expresses itself communally, even within God: Christians recognize in God a trinity of persons, traditionally called the Father, the Son, and the Holy Spirit; it is their self-giving love for one another that, in Dante's words, "moves the sun and other stars."[144]

The basic "sacramental principle" is this: we can know spiritual things through the physical world and bodily actions.

I remember in my sacramental theology class in seminary in the 1960s, old Father Luke teaching us how to baptize. He was quite a rigid type, and was giving us all the things we could do right and wrong in baptizing, yet the only thing he finally insisted on was this: *the water had to flow*. If the water didn't flow at all, if it was not seemingly "living water," people weren't officially baptized. The usual arguments were over the correct words, but without knowing it I think rigid old Father Luke was right.

Baptism is a risky, body-based symbol of being drowned or buried[145] in the flow, and it is most telling that the official formula with almost all churches was insistently Trinitarian. You were not baptized in the name of Jesus, but precisely "*in the name of the Father and of the Son and of the Holy Spirit*," based on Matthew 28:19. Of course, all lives are *objectively* in the flow to begin with, but baptism was ideally the rite of passage coinciding with your *subjective realization* and the beginnings of positive appreciation of the same. As with most sacramental moments, they seldom match the exact moment of transformation itself, but at least they declare that such a moment is important and possible.

And then we have this wonderful body language (a "yoga" of sorts) practiced by the older churches that we call "the sign of the cross." This will be further treated in the "Experiencing the Trinity: Seven Practices" section at the back of the book, but I want to give you a taste of this practice right now. Many of us have been doing this ever since we were little children, while others from other Christian traditions have never done it,

144. Carl McColman, *Befriending Silence: Discovering the Gifts of Cistercian Spirituality* (Notre Dame, IN: Ave Maria Press, 2015), 83–84.
145. See, for example, Romans 6:3–5; Colossians 2:12–13.

believing it extraneous at best and superstitious at worst. If you've never enacted the sign of the cross before, I hope you'll consider its value. And if you're familiar (perhaps overfamiliar) with the practice, I hope you can do it now in a conscious and trustful way.

First of all, the very ritual says that we can know something in our body—that our body has to be reminded in whose "name" it lives and moves and has its being.[146] Some call this "kinesthetic knowing" or even muscle memory. In the centuries and cultures before most people could read or write, this was undoubtedly how most people *knew* reality on a cellular, bodily level.

But let's look at the movement, starting with the head—which is, I think, an unfortunate place to begin, but also notice that we move away from it. *The name of the Father* is the starting place.

And then we pull our hand to our belly, down across our heart and chest. ...*and of the Son* encompasses creation—the physical, the seemingly "lower" material world.

And then we cross this line with the entire world of variety and differentiation from shoulder to shoulder, with...*and of the Holy Spirit*.

The meaning of this embodied gesture is actually quite clear and precise. I now exist under and within a new name—not my Richard name, but my Trinitarian identity. I am marked and signed, indeed!

We stand inside of this wholeness. It really is a marvelous piece of body prayer. Again, if you're not from a tradition that makes this sign, try it. If you're used to doing it in a mindless and perfunctory way, try letting the rote go and breathe through it each step of the way, as I've just shared it. Trinitarian theology has great power to move you out of the head and into the flow, and that is better experienced in our bodies and hearts.

Let me give you another illustration of this. Around the year 2000, near the final days of my Lenten hermitage, and after almost forty days of solitude, the inner flow, happiness, and aliveness became very rich and real for me. I felt like I was being perpetually healed and expanded. I recalled

---

146. See Acts 17:28.

a lesser-known poem of the nineteenth-century priest and poet Gerard Manley Hopkins. In "The Golden Echo," he writes:

> Deliver it, early now, long before death,
> Give beauty back, beauty, beauty, beauty, back to God, beauty's self and beauty's giver.[147]

And in another place:

> This, all this beauty blooming,
> This, all this freshness fuming,
> Give God while worth consuming.[148]

I knew Hopkins was almost perfectly naming my own experience, as should be expected if we were both inhabited by the same wondrous flow. And each remaining morning and evening, I took a long walk down a steep hill and then back up again—but now backward, so I could gaze out with delight at the expansive desert valley in front of me, the various cacti covered with spring flowers. I learned to set my breath to the words of the poem: "*beauty*" on the exhalation and "*back*" on the inhalation, occasionally stopping to recite these verses in their entirety. I did not go to Eucharistic communion most of that Lent; I instead learned to live in communion most of the hours of the day, which I think is the goal of any true sacrament or practice.

This doesn't take a lot of thinking. It doesn't take a lot of theology. It doesn't take a lot of education. It's doesn't even take a lot of morality.

You just have to walk and breathe and receive and give, and—voilà!—you're in the flow. And this cannot be done by just thinking about it.

It's like you're in on the secret of the universe, and yet you can't prove it to anybody, just as I'm likely not "proving" anything to you right now. Even so, stepping into this flow is enough to satisfy you forever. It's enough to make you content with the rest of your life. It's enough to know you *really are okay* and *the world is okay, too*. This is what it means to be captured by the Triune flow.

---

147. http://www.bartleby.com/122/36.html.
148. http://www.bartleby.com/122/24.html.

John of the Cross speaks of being *awakened* by the same delight, *caught* in the same great being, and *breathing* the same air as Jesus.[149]

We can enjoy the same thing that Jesus enjoyed. Why not?

THE MANY BELONG IN THE ONE

Remember that ancient philosophical conundrum we discussed earlier, "the one and the many"?

Most of us don't know how to be diverse and yet one. In unhealthy religion, we've felt this pathological need to make everybody the same; church has become more and more an exclusionary institution instead of this great banquet feast where Jesus constantly invites in "sinners," outcasts, the marginalized, and the ne'er-do-wells.

Jesus says, in effect, "Go out to the highways and the byways—bring everybody in, good and bad alike."

Check it out. Matthew 22. I didn't make that up, all right? It's from Jesus![150]

But we don't like that, do we?

We don't want "those people" in here with us. Maybe send some money or some missionaries "over there" to them, but please don't bring them here, with *us*!

However, our little culture has defined the "bad people" as those *others*, because the ego is much more comfortable with uniformity. People who look like me and talk like me don't threaten my boundaries.

What a contrast to the Trinitarian God who totally releases all claims on such boundaries for the sake of the other! Each member accepts that they're fully accepted by the other.

---

149. See St. John of the Cross, "The Living Flame of Love," stanza 4, in *The Collected Works of St. John of the Cross*, trans. Kieran Kavanaugh, O.C.D. and Otilio Rodriguez, O.C.D. (Washington, DC: ICS [Institute of Carmelite Studies] Publications, 1973), 579. Translation of *Obras de San Juan de la Cruz*. Reprint; previously published in 1964 by Doubleday. "How gently and lovingly You wake in my heart, Where in secret You dwell alone; And in Your sweet breathing, filled with good and glory, How tenderly You swell my heart with love."

150. See also, for example, Matthew 9:9–13; Luke 14:15–24.

This might well be the essence of the spiritual journey for all of us—to accept that we're accepted and to go and live likewise. But we can't do this because we're living out of self-accusation—self-flagellation, in many cases. We're so convinced that we're not the body of Christ, that we're unworthy, that we're disconnected; thus, we've been anesthetized to the good news that the question of union has been resolved once and for all.

You cannot create your union with God; it is objectively already given to you. The only difference between people are those who are consciously drawing upon this union and those who are not.

Let me repeat: The difference is not between those who are united to God and those who aren't. After all, as the psalmist asked,

Where can I go from your Spirit?
Where can I flee from your presence?
If I go up to the heavens, you are there;
if I make my bed in the depths, you are there.[151]

We're all united to God, but only some of us know it. Most of us deny it and doubt it.

It's just—frankly—too good to be true. That's why they call it good news. But it can't be *this* good, can it? Yeah, that's where it gets its name and reputation as *good news*.

Here's a deeper cut on why we're so resistant: to accept that you are accepted is ironically experienced in the first moment (take my word on this) as a loss of power!

The ego wants to be self-made, not other-made, which is our whole problem with grace. If grace is true, dear reader, and if we're all saved by the mercy of God, then why do we constantly try to create certain cutoff points?

We project onto God our way of loving. Our love is determined by the supposed worthiness of a given person: *she's pretty; he's nice.* I, in my magnanimity, will decide to love you because you're so pretty or so nice.

Of course, this has little to do with love, but it *feels* like love, and it's perhaps the first steps toward it. We cannot imagine a love that's not evoked by

---

151. Psalm 139:7–8 (NIV).

the worthiness of the object—and so we try to scrub ourselves up, making ourselves as attractive and worthy as possible.

Dare we throw our religious beauty standards out the window and boldly embrace reality, instead?

God does not love you because you are good. God loves you because God is good.

I should just stop writing right here. There's nothing more to say, and it'll take the rest of your life to internalize this.

Our egoic selves don't know how to wrap around this reality; it feels like a loss of power because—darn it all—there's nothing I can do now to pull myself up and make myself a step ahead of the rest of you!

At that point, that's the ego talking. It wants to prove that it earns this grace—the only problem is, as Paul says in Ephesians 2:4–10, grace is then no longer grace. You have dissolved the entire chemistry of mutuality known as grace in which God always, always, takes the initiative.

Even when you find yourself in a moment desiring to pray, it's because somehow God, in that magnetic center, caught hold of you, and God has already revealed a prayer within you—and you say, "Oh! I think I want to pray." You have to, even at this moment, give thanks to God. It's like a homing device, this Spirit within us, who just keeps sending out the signal to keep redirecting us toward enjoyment of our eternal union.

Whenever you want to love somebody, or forgive somebody, that's your homing device at work—calling you home to that place of communion. It has been said that the universe is not only stranger than we think, but even stranger than we are capable of thinking.[152] Our logic has to break down not only before we can comprehend the nature of the universe, but also the mystery of the Trinity.

Being part of this cosmic dance can only be known experientially. That's why I teach centering prayer and contemplation, and really all intelligent religious rituals and practices: to lead you to a place of nakedness and vulnerability where your ego identity falls away, where your explanations don't mean anything, where your superiority doesn't matter.

---

152. Haldane, "Possible Worlds."

You have to sit there in your naked who-ness.

If God wants to get to you, and the Trinity experience wants to come alive within you, these liminal moments are when God has the very best chance.

ACCESSING THE DIVINE FORCE FIELD

As we "tune our hearts"[153] to greater perception, we'll begin to experience God almost like a force field, to borrow a metaphor from physics (gravitational, electromagnetic, light itself—they all work!). And we're *all already* inside this force field, whether we know it or not, alongside Hindus and Buddhists and every race and nationality. God doesn't stop or begin at the Mexican/American border, the Israel/Palestine border, the border between North and South Korea, or any such line in the sand. These man-made "force fields" pale in energetic strength to the divine force field, which is all-encompassing.

When you see people protecting their small tribes and self-constructed identities as if they were lasting or inherently meaningful, you know that they've not yet experienced substantial reality. When you allow the flow of substantial reality through your life, you are a *catholic* person in the truest sense of the word, a *universal* person living beyond these tiny boundaries that human beings love to create. Paul puts it creatively: *"Our citizenship is in heaven."*[154]

As I grow older, faith for me has become a daily readiness to allow and to trust the force field, knowing that it's good, that it's totally on my side, and that I'm already inside of it. How else can I really be at peace? I've never figured out a long-lasting alternative. Only in a very basic trusting and allowing can I stop fixing things in my mind, even creating mental problems so I have something to work on! The human mind lives inside of such a hamster wheel. Early-twentieth-century teacher P. D. Ouspensky invited us to "divide in [ourselves] the mechanical from the conscious, see how little there is of the conscious, how seldom it works, and how strong is the mechanical: mechanical attitudes, mechanical intentions, mechanical

---

153. In the words of the classic hymn "Come Thou Fount of Every Blessing" by Robert Robinson, 1758.
154. Philippians 3:20 (NIV, NKJV).

thoughts, mechanical desires." Most of our deepest gifts and deepest wounds lie in our unconscious; only prayer forms that touch us there do much good.

A Trinitarian way of entering this invitation would be to renew your mind through the observing awareness of "the Helper" (Spirit) to see what's on autopilot within you, relying on the Father to give you the upgraded consciousness inherent in the mind of Christ![155] Let's try to unpack this.

There are many ways to describe this underlying reality of awareness, letting go, and how to enter the flow. There are so many good teachers emerging today who use different vocabulary, but who each are teaching us how to rest in this quiet holding place that watches the mental commentary rush by and also lets go of it.[156]

Picture this position as the "mercy seat" situated above the ark of the covenant, the portable presence that traveled around with God's people, an open-ended horizon that had to be guarded and protected by two golden cherubim.[157] Such *guarding of presence* is exactly the way that one becomes aware that the force field even exists. You must guard and protect your inner space. This is precisely where YHWH says to Israel, *"I shall come to meet you."*[158] But most have not been taught the practice or the patience to stand guard over this seemingly empty space where your Inner Witnessing Presence, your quiet Inner Knower, dwells. You must learn to trust this Knower. The Spirit is doing the knowing and loving in you, with you, and for you.[159] This is at the heart of a contemplative and truly Christian epistemology. Yet so few know about this already-given gift, even few in formal ministry, it often seems.

Most Christians have not been taught contemplation. *Contemplation* is learning how to *abide in and with* the Witnessing Presence planted within

155. See, for example, Romans 12:2; John 16:3; Philippians 2:5.
156. Several contemporary teachers who teach this well—albeit under various names and precise approaches—would be John Main, Thomas Keating, Pema Chodron, Michael Singer, Eckhart Tolle, Michael Brown in his book *The Presence Process*, and Martin Laird. Each of them can change your life—by practices wherein you know things for yourself, and not by teaching you any doctrines to agree or disagree with.
157. See Exodus 25:10–22 (NKJV, KJV).
158. Exodus 25:22.
159. See Romans 8:26–27.

you, which of course is the Holy Spirit,[160] almost perfectly symbolized by the ark of the covenant. If you keep "guard," like two cherubim, over the dangerous, open-ended space of your transient feelings and thoughts,[161] you will indeed be seated on the mercy seat, where God dwells in the Spirit. The passing flotsam and jetsam on your stream of consciousness will then have little power to trap or imprison you.

The only difference between people that matters is the difference between those who allow this space to fill with flow—and those who don't, or won't, allow it. Like Mary, the model for contemplatives, "it is done unto you,"[162] and you can only allow.

Always.

Just guard the landing field of your own consciousness with your own two golden cherubim, which will often be the two sides of almost any argument. Instead of choosing sides, protect the open space between them, and the Presence will always show itself. These will indeed be "the better angels of your nature" that Abraham Lincoln invoked during the American Civil War. They will allow the emergence of what some call "third force" responses, larger and deeper than the ordinary two sides of most arguments.

Whether as dove, fire, water, or blowing wind, the Third Force of the Holy Spirit will show itself.

You yourself are a traveling ark of the covenant; you hold and guard the space where the Presence shows itself. But the Presence, the Force Field, is already held within you.[163] It only needs allowing and appreciating.

ALWAYS CREATING OTHERNESS

The Spirit's work, if we observe, is always to create and then to fully allow otherness; creating many forms and endless diversity seems to be the plan.

Creating differences, and then preserving them in being.

---

160. See, for example, Romans 8:16.
161. See Philippians 4:6–7.
162. See Luke 1:38 (jb).
163. See John 14:17 and, really, all over the place.

God clearly loves variety. Just when you think you cannot imagine another shape, type, or way of being in this world, you watch the nature channel—or even step outside!—and there is something in the sea, air, or earth that you could never have pictured or imagined.

And then, after God creates this myriad of forms, do you know what God does?

God goes and dwells within them, exposing the inner self of God in every wondrous act of creation—flowing here, loving here, and enjoying here. We name this flowing, creative, inhabiting action *Holy Spirit*, who is precisely the indwelling of God in all things; this is the first and ever-continuing pattern that Christians call the "Incarnation" ("enfleshment"). By our present science, it appears to have begun around thirteen to fourteen billion years ago and is still expanding outward! We now often call it the "Let there be light" moment or "the Big Bang." They are talking about the same thing, one with religious vocabulary seeping over into science, the other with a contemporary metaphor that seeps over into religion.

So Incarnation is not just about Jesus, and then extended somehow to you and me created in the divine image. Genesis even speaks of creation as "complete in all its array,"[164] with God bringing the animals to Adam to give them each a name and thus dignity.[165] Surprisingly, this even precedes the creation of Eve,[166] which I interpret as "the many before any dyads." Remember, Adam is primarily the archetype and stand-in for the whole human race much more than any symbol of masculinity or even a historical male. The split (*sectare* = sex) of gender is preceded by a primal oneness, and the Scripture is not teaching that woman is derivative of man, although I know the text can appear to be saying that.

The significant thing, not much noticed up to now, is that this *"whole creation itself…*[is being] *brought into the same glorious freedom as the children of God"*[167] and is *"groaning in one great act of giving birth."*[168]

---

164. See Genesis 2:1.
165. See Genesis 2:19.
166. See Genesis 2:22.
167. Romans 8:21.
168. Romans 8:22 (JB).

"Born again"…and *again!* is first of all applied to the whole of creation far before it is applied to individuals. This has profound and plentiful implications, of course, not the least of which being that Judeo-Christians should have been the first in line to recognize and honor evolution. The fact that many Christians fought the very idea of evolution shows how small and utterly extrinsic our notion of the Holy Spirit really is. God is still "out there" for most of us.[169]

The irony is that *"all the birds of heaven and all the wild animals"*[170] do not resist, deny, or stop the flow like humans do. They don't appear to say "Oh, I'm a dog; I wish I were a cat." Neither do the *"seed-bearing plants, and fruit trees"*[171] seem to complain about their fate. They willingly accept drought and flood and fire, and the endless recycling of forms that the entire universe is involved in. All accept the flow with the natural inherent grace that humans dismiss as mere "instinct."

All creatures seem to like being what they are and to accept what they're not. But humans, we're a different story, aren't we? We don't like being what we are; and worse, we always want to be someone else. We're mimetic and envious. We've traded our instincts for aspirations, wishing we were thinner, or taller, or more handsome, or whatever, *anything* other than this little incarnation that we are for one gorgeous moment in time. We have a hard time finding grace in "just this"!

All I can give back to God, and all that God wants, is what God has first given to me: this little moment of incarnation, my little "I am" that echoes the great and eternal I AM in grateful awareness.

If God is the great I AM, then we would have to say that evil/Satan is the "I Am Not" who forever accuses others (Satan = the Accuser), denies humans their substance (the "Father of Lies"), and makes negation, opposition, and the creation of separateness his primary task.[172]

---

169. If the idea of a robust, fully Christian embrace and appreciation of evolution intrigues you, or even makes you nervous, I highly recommend that you check out the work of Ilia Delio, especially *The Emergent Christ* (Maryknoll, NY: Orbis Books, 2011) and *The Unbearable Wholeness of Being: God, Evolution, and the Power of Love* (Maryknoll, NY: Orbis Books, 2013).
170. Genesis 2:20.
171. Genesis 1:11.
172. See, for example, Revelation 12:10; John 8:44.

Be reminded that neuroscience now tells us that fear, negativity, and hatred stick like Velcro to the nerves, while positivity, gratitude, and appreciation slide away like Teflon from those same nerves—until we savor them, or choose them, for a minimum of a conscious fifteen seconds! Only then do they imprint![173] Please reflect on this. The positive, loving, and non-argumentative savoring of the moment is called contemplation.

Brazilian liberation theologian Leonardo Boff gives us an invitation to rejoin the great dance—not only of Trinity, but also of creation:

> Creation exists in order to welcome the Trinity into itself. The Trinity seeks to welcome creation within itself.... [Realizing their divinity], men and women will reveal the motherly and fatherly face of God in communion, now including the Trinity with creation and creation with the Trinity.
>
> It is the feast of the redeemed; it is the heavenly dance of those set free. It is the shared life of the sons and daughters in the home and homeland of the Trinity as the Father, the Son, and the Holy Spirit....
>
> *This entire universe, these stars above our head, these forests, these birds, these insects, these rivers, and these stones, everything, everything, is...preserved, transfigured, and made temple of the Blessed Trinity. And we...live in a grand house, as in a single family, minerals, vegetables, animals, and humans with the Father, the Son, and the Holy Spirit. Amen.*[174]

So join me, sisters and brothers, now and for the rest of your life, in allowing this positive flow of Life, marking and blessing your body consciously and slowly—with what is already happening within you:

"In the name of the Father and of the Son and of the Holy Spirit."

Amen.

---

173. See Rick Hanson, *Hardwiring Happiness: The New Brain Science of Contentment, Calm, and Confidence* (New York: Harmony Crown Publishing Group [Penguin Random House], 2013).

174. Leonardo Boff, *Holy Trinity, Perfect Community*, trans. Phillip Berryman (Maryknoll, NY: Orbis Books, 2000), 109–110. Italics are in the original.

NEXT

Before we move on in our exploration of the Trinity, try to be *here*. Which, as you know, is the hardest place to be.

Can you be present to this little bit of *now?*

Get curious: see if you can be present in a positive way, knowing that, reading these words, you're likely carrying the day's events, the day's memories, the day's hurts, and the day's disappointments.

We can let go of these right now, if we choose, because we're going to move into a different kind of knowing, one that the ordinary mind with its ordinary cares simply isn't up for.

Don't be afraid of this silence.

Don't be afraid of what first feels like boredom or nothingness.

Don't be afraid of this silence, which is where God seems to be.

Don't be afraid of this loneliness now and all that it might offer.

Out of this silence, and this hopefully more spacious place, let this prayer resonate in you:

God for us, we call you Father.
God alongside us, we call you Jesus.
God within us, we call you Holy Spirit.
You are the eternal mystery that enables, enfolds, and enlivens all things,
Even us and even me.

Every name falls short of your goodness and greatness.
We can only see who you are in what is.
We ask for such perfect seeing—
As it was in the beginning, is now, and ever shall be.
Amen. (So be it.)[175]

---

175. Richard Rohr, "Trinity Prayer," 2005.

PART II

WHY THE TRINITY? WHY NOW?

THREE REASONS FOR RECOVERY

There are three reasons that make the rediscovery and re-appreciation of Trinity so important and timely at this very moment in history, but these are quite different from the fourth century arguments that made the relations of the Trinity a topic for barroom brawls. (Can you imagine that happening now? Oh, you *have* been to the "Comments" sections of most websites—never mind!)

1. *The Humility of Transcendence.* The human individuation process has come to a very refined sense of interiority, inner experience, psychological sophistication, and interface with what authentic religion is really saying. Up to now, most of the arguing has been about accidentals and externals, which is what Carl Jung criticized in the barren Christianity that was presented to him, an experience echoed in so many others. Trinity offers us a much deeper phenomenology of our inner experience of Transcendence, on a very different plane than the argumentative mind of the last five hundred years. Trinity will change your prayer life, and in fact maybe introduce you to it!

2. *A Broadened Theological Vocabulary.* The globalization of knowledge, our increased interface with other world religions (especially the other hemisphere of the brain represented by both Eastern Christianity and Eastern religions on the whole), along with our new interface with science, all demand that we broaden our theological vocabulary. Ironically, this is leading us back to our oldest tradition of Trinity—this allows us to take each of these new contacts quite seriously while giving us an entirely orthodox way of staying in the full human conversation.

3. *An Expanded Understanding of Jesus and "the Christ."* By essentially extracting Jesus from the Trinity, and attempting to understand Jesus apart from the Cosmic Christ, we have created a very earthbound, atonement-based Christology that will utterly fall apart if and when, for example, we discover life on other planets. We've tried to love Jesus without loving (or even knowing) the Christ, and it has created an unhealthy tribal, competitive form of religion instead of Paul's, *"There is only Christ: he is everything and he is in everything."*[176] "The Christ" is a cosmic and metaphysical statement

---

176. Colossians 3:11.

before it is a religious one. Jesus is a personal and historical statement. Most Christians have the second, but without the first—which has made both Jesus and Christianity far too small.

WHAT HOLDS US BACK FROM GENUINE SPIRITUAL EXPERIENCE?

As we begin to explore our first point, *Transcendence*, this is the premise I am going to ask you to trust here:

An experience that imprints in your memory, or changes you at any depth, is not so much based in *what* you experienced (its content) as it is *how*—at *what level of significance* did you take it in?

Three people can be exposed to the same stimuli and come away with three different "experiences." When you take in events, moments, relationships, and ideas in a readied and vulnerable way, allowing even the Beyond to show itself if it wants to, your likelihood of experiencing the Beyond substantially increases. Even quantum physics and biology now insist that the observer necessarily changes the content and results of an experiment. Our rational mind swears this isn't true, but apparently it is, on a level we are not trained to see. Contemplation is training you to see the overlooked wholeness in all things.

Jesus states the same principle (in reverse!) when he ends one of his stories with this stunning retort to the rich man who wants Lazarus to return from the dead with warning for the living: Father Abraham says, *"They will not be convinced even if someone should rise from the dead."*[177] If you are not open to the Beyond of things, you will not allow yourself to experience a miraculous event happening right in front of you. People who do not believe in miracles never experience miracles. (Do not conclude, however, that people who shout "Miracle!" are always pointing to the Beyond; all too often they are largely pointing to themselves, which might also be okay.)

Let's ground this insight, though, in what we said earlier: our explorations can't be understood with the normal mind. Rather, they are best perceived with what we call the contemplative mind, which is an alternative operating system. *"Deep calls unto deep,"* as the psalmist says.[178]

---

177. Luke 16:31.
178. Psalm 42:7 (NKJV).

Adrienne von Speyr, a twentieth century Swiss Catholic physician and theologian, has a beautiful way of expressing this:

> The Father wants our faith itself to become trinitarian and alive through the manifestation of the Son and the sending forth of the Spirit. He does not want our faith in the Trinity of God to remain two-dimensional and theoretical, nor does he want us to see the one Person only when, and to the extent that, he presents himself, almost as if he were an object contemplated from a distance. Instead, we should be able to perceive each Person revealing himself in his unity with the others and, consequently, in their infinite, divine breadth. This unity...is the expression of love.[179]

Really, it's only God in us that understands the things of God.[180] We must take this very seriously and know how it operates in us, with us, for us, and *as* us. The failure to access our own operating system has kept much Christianity very immature and superficial, filled with secondhand clichés instead of any calm, clear, and immediate experience of reality. It has left us argumentative instead of appreciative.

Most things that we call experience are actually just additions or passing stimulation. To make matters worse, we imprison them inside of the experiences we already have; that's why most people don't grow very much. Most of us then default to one of a handful of templates and filters for all their experiences; everything gets pulled inside of what my little mind already agrees with. This cannot get you very far at all.

Tragically, our cultural default setting is for our inner life to mirror our biology, stopping most growth after age seventeen or eighteen, although I am told there is one more brain surge in the early twenties.

Thus, anything in the realm of mystery—which happens to be, of course, all mature religion, including the idea of the Trinity—remains static in the form of dogma or doctrine, highly abstract, densely metaphysical, and largely irrelevant. Certainly not life-changing unless we allow

---

179. Adrienne von Speyr, *The Boundless God*, trans. Helena M. Tomko (San Francisco: Ignatius Press, 2011), Kindle e-book (locations 469–473), in chapter 5, "The Holy Spirit and How He Paves the Way to the Father."
180. See, for example, 1 Corinthians 2:11–16.

something to cross over, to be a brain-surger and paradigm-shifter. But I am told that on a very good day, most humans are at best willing to call 5 percent of their chosen opinions into question. I hope it is not true.

Do you ever wonder why Western atheism is on the rise? Why does the Christian West, by far, produce the highest number of atheists? What I believe, and have dedicated my life to reversing, is that we have not moved doctrine and dogma to the level of inner experience. As long as "received teaching" doesn't become experiential knowledge, we're going to continue creating a high quantity of disillusioned ex-believers. Or on the flip-side, we'll manufacture very rigid believers who simply hold on to doctrines in very dry, dead ways with nothing going on inside.

And so we have two big groups on the landscape today: those who throw out the baby with the bathwater (many liberals and academics)—and those who seem to have drowned in the bathwater (many conservatives and fundamentalists).

How about allowing the bath water to keep flowing over you and through you?

It is anyway, but we can considerably help the process by gradually opening up the water faucets—both the cold and the hot.

TWO WAYS TO BREAK THROUGH

I might be oversimplifying, but I think there are basically two paths that allow people to have a genuinely new experience: the path of wonder and the path of suffering.

When you allow yourself to be led into awe and wonder, when you find yourself in an *aha!* moment and you savor it *consciously* (remember that joy and happiness take a minimum of fifteen conscious seconds to imprint on your neurons), then you can have a genuinely new experience; otherwise, you will fit everything back into your old paradigm, and it won't really be an *experience* at all. It will at best be a passing diversion, a momentary distraction from your common "cruise control" of thoughts and feelings.

That's all.

Awe and *wonder* are terms that are often correlative with mystery. All fundamentalist religion is terribly uncomfortable with mystery; it likes to take full control of the data, and mystery by definition leaves you out of control. Such moments of vulnerability are the very space where God can most easily break in with fresh experience; in fact, I doubt if God can break through in any other way. Again, in the spiritual world, you can never say with finality, "I know it," or "I've got it all wrapped up." As I wrote in part I, when you come to the end of this little volume, you're certainly not going to be able to say that about the Blessed Trinity. All I'm going to hope to be able to do is circle around this mystery in such a way that invites you to dance, too.

The other path that programs us for genuinely new experience—although at great cost, and with the risk of closing down the soul—is *suffering*.

It must surely be worth the risk, since it comes into every life, necessarily, it seems, and with regularity—*provided* we don't invest in too many insurance policies against it. Hence Jesus' intentionally hyperbolic statements about "rich" people being incapable of understanding his message.

Suffering is the only thing strong enough to break down your control systems, explanatory mechanisms, logical paradigms, desire to be in charge, and carefully maintained sense of control. Both God and the guided soul know to trust suffering, it seems.

God normally has to lead you to the limits of your private resources. Some event, person, or moral situation must force you to admit, *I cannot do this in my present state.* This is our suffering.

Or your understanding of "what it all means" has to fail you in a very personal way: *I can't make sense of this. I can't get through today.*

This often happens when there has been a physical death, or the death of a marriage, a reputation, or an occupation. But you always feel both afraid and trapped. *"How?"* you cry out with ten levels of anguish and impossibility.

A good spiritual director might say quietly to themselves (not to the sufferer), *Hallelujah! Now we're going to begin the real spiritual journey.*

Up to that point, it's merely mental belief systems, mouthing off orthodoxies that mean very little, even to the person themselves. They'd never think of criticizing these feeble beliefs because they're all they have, and some will hang on even more tightly because they don't have any inner experience to ground their beliefs—which is often true of most overstatements and rigorously affirmed beliefs.

Just ask anybody whom you sense truly *knows*—and you'll find out what they know the most is that they don't know anything! This is the giveaway that one has been down at least one of the two paths: wonder or suffering.

When religion returns to this kind of humility, I think we'll see a great lessening of atheism in the West, and a great increase in happy religion.

The Explorer spacecraft, which we sent out in 1977, only in the mid-2000s began moving outside of our heliosphere—the realm of our sun—into massive, seemingly infinite space. Where will its end be? Is there a wall? Who built the wall? The spacecraft has been traveling a million miles a day for decades. It is now approaching the edge of our heliosphere, and yet it will be forty thousand years before it again approaches another galaxy.

Who is this God? What is this God up to? How can any of my words point to anything real or understandable to the human mind?

Again, those who are looking through microscopes and those who are looking through telescopes are seeing this same pattern: if reality is anything, it's absolutely relational. It's orbital somehow, mostly empty space, and even much of that is dark matter or black holes—none of it fully subject to our control. Then mystics like Teilhard de Chardin come along and teach that "the [very] physical structure of the universe is love."[181] All this orbiting, exploding, expanding, and even contracting is Infinite Love at work.[182]

Everything you have ever seen with your eyes is the self-emptying of God into multitudinous physical and visible forms.

---

181. See Pierre Teilhard de Chardin, "Sketch of a Personal Universe," trans. J. M. Cohen, in *Human Energy* (New York: Harcourt Brace Jovanovich, 1962), 72, https://cac.org/the-shape-of-the-universe-is-love-2016-02-29/.
182. Again, we should probably end this book right here! What else is there to say?

In other words, Infinity is forever limiting itself into finite expressions, and this could even be called the "suffering" of God. The Christ learned this self-emptying, or *kenosis*,[183] from his eternal life in the Trinity. It is not just Jesus who suffers, but the cross is the visible symbol of what is always going on inside of God!

Think on this. It should be enough to make anyone love the Christian message.

No one would want to opt out of such love, would they?

Yet many of our young people, and many of our old people, too, are not having it. They're leaving the right-belief systems of their parents and grandparents in droves. This is a mass exodus from institutional faith that demographers are calling "the rise of the Nones." Nones comprise about 20 percent of all Americans, and one-third of Americans under thirty.[184] A Pew Research Center study says that "while 42% of the [religiously] unaffiliated describe themselves as neither a religious nor a spiritual person, 18% say they are a religious person, and 37% say they are spiritual but not religious."[185]

Having little patience with (or appreciation for) mystery, as well as so little humility or basic love for groups other than our own (never mind nonhuman creation), maybe our Christian religion in its present formulation *has* to die for a truly cosmic and love-centered spiritual path to be born. I sincerely wonder if this might be true.

SUFFERING'S SURPRISING SUSTENANCE

We're spending this entire book exploring the path of love and wonder; let's take just one more section to fully dive into suffering, shall we? I know it isn't likely your favorite topic—unless you're a masochist!—but I think an understanding of suffering love can be quite valuable to you as you reflect on your own pain. I make no promises, but you just might discover meaning—and redemption—in what you've gone through.

183. See Philippians 2:7.
184. James Emery White, *The Rise of the Nones: Understanding and Reaching the Religiously Unaffiliated* (Baker, 2014), 21.
185. See http://www.pewforum.org/2012/10/09/nones-on-the-rise-religion/.

Trinitarian spirituality leads us to an open-handed embrace of the whole—no exceptions. This is the circle of freedom, certainly, but it's *also* a circle of suffering. The negative side dare not be eliminated.[186] Everything belongs.

As a first-century letter to friends of God puts it:

> *Praise be to the God and Father of our Lord Jesus Christ, the Father of compassion and the God of all comfort, who comforts us in all our troubles, so that we can comfort those in any trouble with the comfort we ourselves receive from the Spirit. For just as we share abundantly in the sufferings of Christ, so also our comfort abounds through Christ.*[187]

Can you see the entirety of the Trinitarian worldview at work here? This letter was penned about the year 58 CE. The theology of Trinity hadn't yet been developed; it took three centuries for us to do this. But here Paul, a first-rate mystic, already intuits the whole thing. He is already addressing all three of the persons of the Trinity as magnetic Sources that are drawing and naming his experience.

In the Pauline school, the letter to the Colossians further speaks of our power to contribute back to this circle of eternal consolation and eternal suffering:

> *Now I rejoice in what I am suffering for you, and I fill up in my flesh what is still lacking in regard to Christ's afflictions, for the sake of his body, which is the church.*[188]

What's he talking about? Clearly, he's involved in a participatory mystery that's drawing him in. Formerly, when I read lives of the mystics, I thought they were always praying to feel some of Jesus' suffering. They're always depicted holding, or looking at, a crucifix. I frankly thought most of them were sadomasochists!

But I was wrong; I misunderstood these mystics. They can only be understood by someone who is in the dance. Let me give you two examples.

---

186. See Rohr, *Eager to Love*, chapter 7, "The Franciscan Genius: The Integration of the Negative."
187. 2 Corinthians 1:3–5 (NIV).
188. Colossians 1:24 (NIV).

The first is Teresa of Ávila, the sixteenth-century Spanish Carmelite teacher who was named a Doctor of the Church by Pope Paul VI in 1970 due to her keen insight and spirit for reform. She said this:

> My soul began to enkindle, and it seemed to me I knew clearly in an intellectual vision that the entire Blessed Trinity was present... all three Persons were represented distinctly in my soul and that they spoke to me, telling me that from this day I would see an improvement in myself in respect to three things and that each one of these Persons would grant me a favor: one, the favor of charity; another, the favor of being able to suffer gladly; and the third, the favor of experiencing this charity with an enkindling in the soul.... It seems those three Persons, being only one God, were so fixed within my soul that I saw that were such divine company to continue it would be impossible not to be recollected.[189]

This communion, participation, and solidarity with the mystery becomes so deep that a second exemplar, Etty Hillesum, wrote to this effect while she was at Westerbork transit camp, before her ultimately fatal captivity in Auschwitz: *I somehow want to suffer with you, God. All this suffering is somehow your suffering, and I want to participate with you in it.*[190]

We all find ourselves falling tragically short of abundant life, in spite of all our comfort-seeking. We find, much to our disappointment, that there's nothing in it. We all eventually discover that our hearts and souls will not be fed at the trough of self-seeking.

God is not "once upon a time"—God is "the never-ending story" in which we are scripted![191]

This is scary-good news, from which we can consciously draw freedom and meaning. It seems we can actually cooperate with God, creating spaces of freedom in the heart of the world. Paul even spoke of it as "working together with," or co-creation.[192] When she was at Westerbork in the midst of

---

189. Anne Hunt, *The Trinity: Insights from the Mystics* (Collegeville, MN: Liturgical Press, 2010), 136.
190. For more on this remarkable woman, see *Etty Hillesum: Essential Writings*, Modern Spiritual Masters (Maryknoll, NY: Orbis Books, 2009).
191. See Hebrews 12:2 (NKJV, KJV), and of course *The Neverending Story* by Michael Ende (New York: Puffin Books, 1979).
192. See Romans 8:28.

tremendous suffering, Etty Hillesum lived an astonishing existence of peace, love, and communion with God. She created little spaces of freedom for herself and for others. She found the deepest meaning of life.

This is full reality, so full it can include the downside. Etty Hillesum was completely operating in God, and even as God, in her suffering. She was full-blown in the cycle of the mystery, drawn into a life larger than her own. She might not even have understood why she would think or say such an illogical thing as *I somehow want to suffer with you, God.* It's not that we masochistically seek pain or suffering, but when we encounter suffering, we find our capacity growing if we stay connected to the flow. Obviously, even then we have to block out a certain degree of raw suffering for self-care. We can't take it all in, but apparently God can. That's the visual of the cross—God taking in all the pain of history. You don't have to take it all in, but don't block it entirely. Let pain bring its gift of vulnerability. Let some of it change you. Let some of it call you outside your comfort zone to this bigger place where we all are one. In a way, *there is only one suffering and one cosmic sadness, and it is the very suffering of God. And we all share in it.*

Such an empathetic plunge into solidarity with God and humanity can never proceed from mere theological theory; it has been seen by many saints as a vocation, an invitation, and even a privilege.

I find this solidarity even more impressive when heard through the voices of those who didn't at first take it up as a vocation and certainly not from a place of privilege, those who instead found themselves in social situations where the dominant culture left them disempowered—even oppressed. Listen to this articulation of the Divine Dance from the "underside":

> As beloved triune community, God "dances" to birth human communities torn by suffering, hatred, and division. God empathizes with the oppressed in "blues-filled" experiences and directs their anger creatively and constructively for the sake of justice. In particular, the Spirit who hovered in creation from the beginning of the world is the creative and "life-inspiring relation of God" that makes "a way out of no way possible." "She" is the relational action of God sent "to create beauty out of ugliness, celebrate life in the midst of suffering, and walk in love in the midst of hate." As the

life-giving relation, the Spirit prophetically seeks to realize human societies in the image of God.[193]

Trinity is the all-in-all God and is thus everywhere without exception; if God could be said to have a *favorite* place, however, it is always in solidarity with the "other"—those on the margins of power. Black Liberation theologian James Cone puts it provocatively:

God is black...God is mother...God is rice...God is red.

The blackness of God implies that essence of the nature of God is to be found in the concept of liberation. Taking seriously the Trinitarian view of the Godhead, black theology says that as Creator, God identified with oppressed Israel, participating in the bringing into being of this people; as Redeemer, God became the Oppressed One in order that all may be free from oppression; as Holy Spirit, God continues the work of liberation. The Holy Spirit is the Spirit of the Creator and the Redeemer at work in the forces of liberation in our society today.[194]

Do we—especially those of us located in a more privileged place—dare accept this? If we are Trinitarian, I say we must; God's humility calls for it. What absolute freedom to join the Beloved wherever he is—especially in beloved community, living out the good struggle for increased dignity, harmony, creativity, and liberation. We know that, during his entire life on earth, Jesus went wherever the pain was; his apprentices only follow him.

AT-ONE-MENT

Sometimes I court controversy because we Franciscans never explained God's at-one-ment with humanity in terms of the current popular

---

193. Miguel H. Díaz, "The Life-giving Reality of God from Black, Latin American, and US Hispanic Theological Perspectives," in *The Cambridge Companion to the Trinity*, ed. Peter C. Phan (Cambridge: Cambridge University Press, 2011), 263. Diaz draws from Karen Baker-Fletcher's excellent *Dancing with God: The Trinity from a Womanist Perspective* (St. Louis, MO: Chalice Press, 2006).
194. James H. Cone, "God Is Black," in *Lift Every Voice: Constructing Christian Theologies from the Underside*, ed. Susan Brooks Thistlethwaite and Mary Potter Engel, rev. ed., 101–114 (Maryknoll, NY: Orbis Books, 2001), 103.

atonement theory that some theologians call "penal substitution." We never did, since the thirteenth-century debates on the same.

Please understand that I'm not questioning God's redemptive work in and through Jesus Christ; I'm only questioning a particular interpretation of it that was virtually unheard of in our ancient past but seems to pick up steam over the millennia.

I think penal substitution is a very risky theory, primarily because of what it implies about the Father's lack of freedom to love or to forgive his own creation.

It is already an uphill climb to get people to trust the infinite love of God, and this does not help at all. I know this from years of directing souls. Any "transactional" explanation of salvation keeps people from the oh-so-necessary transformation into trust and love that we all desperately need. *Humans change in the process of love-mirroring, and not by paying any price or debt.* This lifeless, transactional approach is a direct and unfortunate corollary to pulling Jesus out of the fountain fullness of the Holy Trinity!

The cross is the standing icon and image of God, showing us that God knows what it's like to be rejected; God is in solidarity with us in the experience of abandonment; God is not watching the suffering from a safe distance. Somehow, believe it or not, God is *in* the suffering with us.

God is not only stranger than we thought, but stranger than we're capable of thinking! But we tried to pull salvation into some kind of quid pro quo logic and justice theory—and retributive justice at that! God's justice, revealed in the prophets, is always *restorative* justice, but this takes a transformed consciousness to understand. Read, for example, Ezekiel 16:53–55 where, after reaming out the people of Israel, Ezekiel uses the word "*restore*" four times in a row, and then "*restored*" three more times. God "punishes" Israel by loving them even more and at even deeper levels, just as God does with every human soul. This is the biblical theme of restorative justice, but it was just too countercultural to be heard above the nonstop historical drumbeat of retributive justice.

The quid pro quo, retributive mind has to break down in order to truly move forward with God. This is the unique job description of grace and undeserved mercy. Mystics are people who allow this new calculus, but it is always an act of surrender and falling. Ezekiel says that Israel will feel *"ashamed,"* "confused," and *"reduced to silence"* when God forgives them for everything they have done.[195] Grace and mercy are always a humiliation to the ego. We must accept God's knowing and loving as the full and final shape of goodness. But you must know that, to the ego, this first feels like losing; and to the "counting" mind, it feels like undeserved mercy. Basically, we have to stop counting, measuring, and weighing.

Let me paraphrase 1 John 4:10 in this way: love consists in this—not limiting God by our human equations of love, but allowing God's infinite love to utterly redefine our own.

Whenever we love, we are in some way participating in the very suffering of God, the necessary self-emptying that must precede and make room for every infilling. Yes, we must offer our lives opposing human and planetary suffering, I hope. But paradoxically, we embrace suffering as one vital form of participating in the mystery of the Incarnate One and the healing of the world.

We want to take away suffering whenever we can, and we want to lessen human pain whenever possible. We certainly don't want to impose it, although we all know that we do increase the suffering in the world through our sin and mutual alienation. But somehow, after we've done all we can to try to alleviate suffering according to our gifts and callings, we find that we're led to embracing what is, embracing what is left—and this is often suffering and pain, is it not?

Maybe this is the great death, this third space where I refuse to waste the rest of my years in either fight or flight. Where I give up the search for someone to hate or to blame—myself or anybody else. I'm going to somehow enter into solidarity with this pain. I'll not allow myself to participate in other people's abandonment, betrayal, rejection, or marginalization.

That's why the saints, the Trinitarian believers, always find ourselves going to the edge, going to the bottom, going to those who are excluded at the margins. Jesus is constantly going to the lepers and those whom society labels "sinners." How could he have made it any clearer than he did? Once we see this, it becomes much harder for us to fall into that ancient, ubiquitous fear that God causes suffering, which has always been an intellectual stumbling block.

---

195. See Ezekiel 16:63.

On a cross, we find this man who has given his whole life to heal suffering becoming a victim of suffering himself. Instead of being a torturer, a murderer, a tyrant, or an oppressor, Jesus shares in the victimization of humanity; and it's here that even Jesus experiences his own resurrection. He neither plays the victim nor creates victims. This lays the third path of redemptive suffering before history and eternity.

Jesus himself dies and is reborn in this transformative place. The word that most describes this total dynamic of being given to and giving back with total vulnerability on each side is, ironically, the word *forgiveness*.

No wonder two-thirds of Jesus' teaching is directly or indirectly about forgiveness!

To forgive, you have to be able to see the other person—at least momentarily—as a whole person, as an image of the Divine, containing holiness and horror at the same time. In other words, you can't eliminate the negative. You know they've hurt you. You know they did something wrong.

You have to learn to live well with paradox, or you can't forgive. The trouble with so much conventional religion is this cultural attitude of, "Well, I'll forgive when they've earned it, when they've proven themselves."

That's not forgiveness—that's a deal!

God loves you precisely in your obstinate unworthiness, when you're still a mixture of good and bad, when you're gloriously in flux. You're not a perfectly loving person, and God still totally loves you.

When you can participate in that mystery of being loved, even as the mixed bag that you are, you can receive the gift of the forgiveness. And as far as I'm concerned, that's the only magnetic center that knows how to forgive other people—especially when people have really screwed you, really betrayed you, really abandoned you, really humiliated you. And sooner or later, this happens to all of us.

This is why the Franciscans have rejected the whole "forensic" notion of atonement—it not only does violence to the character of God, but it's also overly sanitized against messy reality, it's an abstraction against immediacy. The whole shattering experience of living is avoided whenever we try to make forgiveness into mere legal pardon—like Catholic indulgences or confession, or Protestant transactional theories of salvation. Such an approach reflects a mind-set of, "Let's *do* something. Let's avoid this whole relational vulnerability thing if we can, okay? Let's just skip out on confidence and surrender."

This kind of religion is not Trinitarian. It's not participating in the divine dance, and it's not going to get us anywhere. When I can stand under the waterfall of infinite mercy and know that I am loved precisely in my unworthiness, then I can easily pass along mercy to you.

Check each day how you're doing with forgiveness, all right? That's as good a test as any I can think of to see if you're living inside the incalculable mystery of divine generosity.

Do you know what's even harder to forgive? It's often the petty things, the accumulating resentments. The little things you know about another person; how they sort of did you wrong yesterday. No big deal, but the ego loves to grab onto those; they build up on the psyche like a repetitive stress injury. I think that in many ways, it's much harder to let go of these micro-offenses, precisely because they're so tiny. And so we unconsciously hoard them, and they clog us up.

But God is not transactional, and God is not needy. You can trust that God is treating you as you would wish to be treated—letting go of your pettiness, your silliness, your judgmentalism, and your blockages to love— while *still* seeing you as whole.[196]

God cannot *not* see his Son Jesus in you. You are the body of Christ. You are bone of God's bone, and that's why God cannot stop loving you. That's why no amount of effort will make God love you any more than God loves you right now. And despite your best efforts to be terrible, you can't make God love you any less than God loves you right now.

You are in a position of total powerlessness, and your ego is fighting it. All you can do is surrender and enter into this dance of unhindered dialogue, this circle of praise, this web of communion that we call the Blessed Trinity.

From the beginning of this attempt to unravel the mystery of Trinity, I have been astounded by the ability of this doctrine, which appeared so

---

196. See 1 Corinthians 13:5.

abstruse, rarified, distant, and even meaningless, to transport us to a different universe.

It's a different-shaped Christianity. It's a different-shaped cosmology, as it should be if this is the shape of all things, not only of God but of everything else.

WHAT ABOUT THE WRATH OF GOD?

So where is wrath in a Trinitarian God? You probably grew up hearing passages about God's wrath from the Hebrew Scriptures (the Christian Old Testament); and even Paul refers to "the wrath of God."[197] Therefore you rightly say, "Well, why are there such passages in Holy Writ?"

Why, indeed? In certain biblical narratives, God seems to be upset for a few days. God isn't loving us, it appears. And of course, that's understandably our reading of our own experience, finding language for what our lineage eventually names "dark nights of the soul"—those periods where we're not experiencing the grace, love, and given-ness of existence. We project this all onto God; isn't it obvious?

This doesn't mean, of course, that the divine given-ness is not objectively here. It is just that we are not drawing upon it. For whatever reason, we're not accessing it, enjoying it, or participating in it. Scripture, as Peter Enns so artfully put it, is *also* fully human and fully divine.[198] Scripture is always, always written by humans from a human perspective. We call it the "word of God," but the only Word of God unequivocally endorsed in the Bible's pages is Jesus, the eternal Logos. The words on our inspired pages are the words of men and women.

In my book *Things Hidden: Scripture as Spirituality*, I describe the Bible itself as a gradual progression forward.[199] You see the narrative arc moving toward an ever-more-developed theology of grace, until Jesus becomes grace personified. But it's a concept that the psyche is never fully ready for. We resist it, and so you'll see in most of the biblical text what the late anthropologist

---

197. See, for example, Romans 1:18 (NIV, NKJV, KJV); Ephesians 5:6 (NIV, NKJV, KJV).
198. See Peter Enns, *Inspiration and Incarnation: Evangelicals and the Problem of the Old Testament*, 2nd ed. (Grand Rapids, MI: Baker Academic, 2015).
199. Richard Rohr, *Things Hidden: Scripture as Spirituality* (Cincinnati, Ohio: St. Anthony's Messenger Press/Franciscan Media, 2010).

Rene Girard calls a "text in travail," a suffering text. And we must see that is still true in the New Testament, where even John's statements about God's unconditional love are still interspersed with many lines that seem to imply a conditional love, too: "*If you obey my commandments*" is either directly said or implied many times. To grow in the ways of love, I think this shows real genius. Psychologically, humans actually need some conditional love to lead us toward the recognition of and the need for unconditional love. This is much of my assumption in my book *Falling Upward*.[200]

We get the promise of free love (grace) now and then, but it is always too much for the mind and heart to believe.

The biblical text mirrors both the growth and the resistance of the soul.

It falls into the mystery, and then it says, "That just can't be true." Scripture is a polyphonic symphony, a conversation with itself, where it plays melodies and dissonance—three steps forward, two steps back. The three steps gradually and finally win out; you see the momentum of our Holy Book and where it is leading history. And the text moves inexorably toward inclusivity, mercy, unconditional love, and forgiveness. I call it the "Jesus hermeneutic." Just interpret Scripture the way that Jesus did! He ignores, denies, or openly opposes his own Scriptures whenever they are imperialistic, punitive, exclusionary, or tribal. Check it out for yourself.[201]

---

200. Richard Rohr, *Falling Upward* (San Francisco: Jossey-Bass, 2011).

201. Here are but a few examples: First, in Luke 4:18–19 (NIV), when Jesus reads from the Isaiah scroll, beginning with, *"The Spirit of the Lord is upon me, because he has anointed me to proclaim good news to the poor..."* and ending his reading with *"to proclaim the year of the Lord's favor,"* he leaves off *"and the day of vengeance of our God"* as it is in the original passage. (See Isaiah 61:1–2.) Then, rather than proclaim foreigners as the enemies and objects of God's vengeance, Jesus turns around and praises faithful foreigners from Zarephath and Syria, while reproaching the attitudes of his own fellow "chosen" people. The people become so angry at his selective reading that they try to throw him off a cliff! (See Luke 4:25–30.) For more examples like this, see Michael Hardin's *The Jesus Driven Life: Reconnecting Humanity with Jesus*, rev. and exp. edition (Lancaster, PA: JDL Press, 2013), particularly chapter 2, "How Jesus Read His Bible." For a powerful, semi-fictionalized telling, see Jack Miles's Pulitzer Prize-winning *Christ: A Crisis in the Life of God* (New York: Knopf, 2001). Additionally, in Matthew 5, in Jesus' well-known Sermon on the Mount, he begins a series of teachings with, *"You have heard that it was said...,"* summarizing a key, accepted part of the Law, and contrasting it with *"But I say to you...,"* bringing his own—often subversive—take on it. For more on the sweepingly different vision of Jesus' most well-known message, see my own *Jesus' Plan for a New World: The Sermon on the Mount* (Cincinnati, OH: St. Anthony Messenger Press, 1996). For still more examples, see Matthew 12:1–8 and John 5:1–23.

This is why the Bible is the best book in the world, and if we're honest, it has often been the *worst* book in the world—not because of its content but because of the spiritual maturity of those reading it. In the hands of loveless fundamentalists, it could be credited with more rigidity, bigotry, hatefulness, war, evil, and killing than almost any other book on this planet. You know that is true. It is only comfortable people in the dominant group who do not see this now.

St. Thomas Aquinas taught that the corruption of the best is the worst. So the Bible is capable of great good, but we all understand it at our own stage of emotional and spiritual development. If you are still a black-and-white, rigid thinker who needs certitude and control at every step—well, the Trinity will feel out of reach. Grace shows up where logic breaks down, so you won't go very far. No matter what passage is given to you, you will interpret it in a stingy, vengeful, controlling way—because that's the way you do life.

Trinity gradually becomes real for you as you honestly enter into the cycles and flow of life and death yourself. This is what we mean when we say "we are saved by the death and resurrection of Jesus." Exactly! First of all, we have to grow up, which is largely learning how to live on the waterwheel of giving and receiving love. Quite simply, when you've found the flow *in here*, you'll see it *over there*. We call this the Principle of Likeness.

Hateful people see hatred everywhere else, have you noticed that? They're always thinking someone's out to screw them over, someone's trying to hurt them. They create problems wherever they go. We call them "high-maintenance" people.

On the other hand, certain people come up to me and say, "Oh, Richard, you're just so loving." How I wish I were! I love intermittently, it's true, on my better days; but invariably, people who say this to me are themselves very loving people! In that complimentary moment, they're pulling it out of me.

People accuse me of all kinds of things, both wonderful and terrible. They're usually half-right, of course. But invariably, they're talking about themselves, and they can't see it. This principle of likeness has positive and negative manifestations—what you see *over there* is what you are *in here*.

Always. Mistrustful people don't know how to trust themselves or anybody else, and so they lay it on you.

The Trinity beautifully undoes this negativity by a totally, totally—and we can't emphasize the *totally* enough—a *totally* positive movement that never reverses its direction.

Our mixed pattern of forward and backward is illustrated throughout the Bible, which often reverses its direction or undoes itself. After awhile, you will spot this naturally. But the Divine Generosity is *not* undone in the Trinity, who only gives.

God is *always* giving, even in those moments when we momentarily experience the inaccessibility of love as if it were divine anger. When you find yourself drawing these conclusions, be close to your soul for a moment. You are angry at yourself in that moment. All of us probably go through that at least twice a day. *Why did I do that?* we accuse ourselves—or blame it on God. Really!

How can you get out of this vicious cycle? Own your projections—those onto other people, those onto your own motives, and perhaps especially those onto God. In reality, God is the divine lure who is most equipped to pull you out of this circle of negativity. But if you ascribe negativity onto God, too, you're really in trouble spiritually because you've got no way out now, without traversing Kubler-Ross's first four stages of both grief and dying—denial, anger, bargaining, and depression—before you can get to the fifth stage, which is divine acceptance.

This now-evident pattern is why so many of our contemporary spiritual teachers say that most of our problems are psychological in their manifestation, but spiritual in their solution. Most Christians of the Middle Ages more easily trusted the spiritual solution than we do, but they seldom had the vocabulary to describe the psychological manifestations as we do today. We articulate the psychological dimensions so well, and in so many ways, that contemporary people are trapped in sophisticated and helpful descriptions of the manifestations but have no One to surrender it all to. There is no Receiver Station, because we jumped off the divine waterwheel and withdrew from the dance.

To sum it all up, I do not believe there is any wrath in God whatsoever—it's theologically impossible when God is Trinity.

EXPANDING OUR HORIZONS

Our second point in exploring "Why the Trinity? Why Now?" concerns a movement toward a broadened theological vocabulary. If you don't mind, I'm going to take some hints about Trinity from outside of Christianity. In our highly polarized religious climate, I understand that some Christians have been taught for generations to be afraid of anything that doesn't come "purely" from "our" sources. Ironically enough, our own Scripture contains ample examples of appreciative appraisal of elements of neighboring faiths, whether it's Eastern pagan astrologers accurately divining the birth of the Christ child and worshipping him,[202] syncretistic-heterodox Samaritans being the heroes of parable and encounter,[203] Greek philosophy offering us its concept of *logos*,[204] or approving citations of neo-Platonic poetry as pointing to the all-in-all nature of the one true God![205]

We are fearful; God, apparently, is fearless.

If the truth is the truth...if God is one...then there's one reality and there's one truth.[206] You'd think we'd be happy when other religions deduce approximately the same thing, wouldn't you? But oh, sometimes we get so upset. We don't know how to recognize friends, and we create enemies for no good reason.

Hinduism is probably the oldest still-existing religion on earth, its foundation going back five millennia. In Hindu theology and in the Hindi language, there are three qualities of God—and therefore, of all reality. I

---

202. See Matthew 2:1–12.
203. See Luke 10:25–37 for the parable of the Good Samaritan; see John 4:4–41 for the account of Jesus' encounter with the Samaritan woman at the well, wherein they discuss some of the theological differences between Orthodox Jews and heterodox Samaritans, with Jesus ultimately pointing to a place of Spirit and reality that transcends both of their social and spiritual locations.
204. See John 1:1–5; 1 John 1:1–3.
205. See Acts 17:16–34.
206. See Ephesians 4:4–6.

heard these words frequently when I was teaching in India some years ago: *sat, chit, ananda.*

I won't even have to work hard to make the Trinitarian point here; it's obvious, I am sure:

Sat is the word for "being." God is being itself; it's hard to get more expansive than that. Hinduism seemed to implicitly recognize this, exactly as Paul says to the Athenians in his aforementioned stump speech at Mars Hill.[207] Universal Being, the Source of all being, whom we call Father.

Chit is the word for consciousness or knowledge. God is consciousness itself, mind itself, awareness itself. Does that sound anything like *logos*? It should. Of course, our biblical concept of *logos* was drawn from Greek philosophy; the writer of the gospel of John has already done what I'm doing now, drawing from extra-biblical (and extra-Judaic) wisdom.[208] Now more than ever, we have to draw from our shared spiritual heritage to better understand our own belief.

And, finally, *ananda.* I met a number of people named Ananda in India. It means *happiness*—*bliss* is the way Indians usually translate it. Does this sound like the joy of the Holy Spirit? Inherent, uncreated happiness, which is what you experience when you live without resistance inside the flow. It's omnidirectional, not determined by any one object that makes you happy. You don't know where it came from, just as Jesus said of the Spirit.[209] You can't capture it, predict it, or prove it; you can only enjoy it when the dove descends, the wind blows, the fire falls, or the water flows. Like grace itself, *ananda* is always a gift from "nowhere."

Sat-chit-ananda.

Being-knowledge-happiness.

Father-Son-Spirit.

Truth is one, and universal.

---

207. See Acts 17:28 for the key phrase in Paul's message.
208. Compare the development of the idea of *logos* beginning with the sixth-century BCE philosopher Heracleitus through Jesus' first-century CE context. For a very basic overview, see www.britannica.com/topic/logos.
209. See John 3:8.

SILENCE: FATHER

The Father is Being itself, the Source of the flow, the Creator—the formless One out of which all form comes. God as "nothingness," unspeakable Mystery.[210]

In our contemplative heritage, God the Father is normally experienced best in silence, beyond words or pronunciation, which is exactly what the Jewish people insisted upon.[211] This preserves our humility before God so we don't think that any word will ever comprehend the divine incomprehensibility.[212]

In the long tradition of Christian mysticism, there were two great strains of knowing that were both needed to keep the believer balanced, humble, and open.

The first way of knowing, which was more commonly practiced, was called the *kataphatic* (seen according to light) or the "positive" way—relying on defined words, clear concepts, pictures, and rituals. Christ as Logos, image, and manifestation embodies this *kataphatic*, or *via positiva*, pole.

And when religion is healthy, happy, and mystical, the way of light needs to be balanced by the *apophatic* (against the light) or "negative" way of darkness—knowing beyond words and images through silence, darkness, open space, and releasing the need to know. This *via negativa* is represented by the Ground of Being, or "Father."

The apophatic has largely disappeared in the last five hundred years; almost all congregations, parishes, and ordinary Christians are entirely kataphatic. This has resulted in an eclipse of the "Father."

The great spiritual teachers always balance knowing with not-knowing, light with darkness. Both ways are necessary, and *together* they create a magnificent form of higher non-dual consciousness called faith. I see this energy between—the healthy interplay between kataphatic and apophatic—as where the Spirit shows up to play.

---

210. The concept of God as the "negative space" from which all creation pours forth is a rich dimension worthy of a book of its own. For just a taste, try out exercise number 5, "Seeing (in the Dark)," in the appendix of this book.
211. See Exodus 20:7.
212. See Richard Rohr, *The Naked Now* (Crossroad, New York, 2009), particularly chapter 2.

Unfortunately, this dynamism is not often present. The apophatic has almost always been in the minority, as we in civilization are uncomfortable with silence, wonder, and not-knowing. Only the mystics preserved this apophatic path, along with some of the sacramental traditions in worship. But even these were suspect by Protestants who threw out the mystical and sacramental baby with the medieval Catholic bathwater, although the Quakers have certainly tried to recover a uniquely Protestant sense of mysticism, along with a perspective that all of life is sacramental—that is, as an outward sign of inward divine presence.

Most of us do not know the ground of silence before speaking, the spaciousness around words, the inner repose after words, the humility that words should require. This was instinctual for our ancient ancestors before the advent of organized agriculture, cities, and civilization—and it is still much more strongly present in First Nations and indigenous cultures where these ancient instincts are better tended.[213]

This is the realm of "the Father"—who cannot be spoken, who cannot be named. God named Father is precisely the Un-manifest, the Great Silence, the Unspeakability of God. We were so anxious to speak words that were infallible and inerrant that we bet all our money on words to get us there, even forgetting that words themselves are always metaphors.

We basically repressed God the Father, whose reputation had already been seriously tarnished by unhealthy patriarchy in general, and penal substitutionary atonement theory in particular, where he became completely unfree, incapable of forgiveness, bound by a very limited notion of justice—and frankly petty and punitive. We feared the Father more than loved him. This loss alone is enough to reveal why Christianity needs to rediscover all three persons of the Trinity anew, along with the entire "apophatic trinity" of humility, darkness, and silence.

Don't think that this metaphor "Father" is trying to ascribe gender to God. God is not masculine. That's not the point. It simply became the classic term because *Abba* is the word that Jesus used to connote safety

---

213. This is why the work of initiation in the world today owes an ongoing debt of gratitude to these indigenous and First Nations peoples; to witness a breathtaking look at Christ's incarnation from an indigenous, initiatory perspective, read *The Four Vision Quests of Jesus* by Steven Charleston (New York: Morehouse Publishing, 2015).

and endearment. It is actually a child's word, closest to *Papa* or *Daddy*. But unfortunately, it suffers today from centuries of being heard (and used) inside patriarchal cultures, implicitly validating a hierarchical worldview.

The Abba-Father of Jesus, by contrast, is much more moving inside a circle than at the top of any pyramid. Read Sandra Schneiders's now classic small study *Women and the Word*, where she very effectively demonstrates that Jesus probably had to come in a male body to undo any patriarchal notion of God from the inside out.[214]

Of course, the mind is humbled before such unnameability, such incomprehensibility, as we recognize again that all metaphors limp.

In the first metaphor offered to Moses, YHWH refuses all picture words. Moses, barefoot and astonished, asks, "Give me your name."

The Unnameable One replies, "I AM WHO I AM."[215]

There are probably ten good ways to translate that. I'm not saying this is the perfect one, but basically, this One says, "It's none of your business. Don't you try to capture me by a name. Don't you try to contort me into any little box. I will be who I will be."

It's the great Jewish tetragrammaton, which we're lucky to have right over our St. Francis cathedral in my home near Santa Fe: יהוה

It is, I believe, the only cathedral entrance in America that has it right above the door: *I Am Who I Am*. During the cathedral's construction in the nineteenth century, Archbishop Jean-Baptiste Lamy put it there in honor of and respect for the Jewish tradition and people.

In some ways, the prayer that we let resonate in us earlier and that we continue to explore through this book sums up everything I want to say here:

> God for us, we call you Father.
> God alongside us, we call you Jesus.
> God within us, we call you Holy Spirit.
> You are the eternal mystery that enables, enfolds, and enlivens all things,
> Even us and even me.

---

214. See Sandra Schneiders, *Women and the Word* (New York: Paulist Press, 1986), 50ff.
215. Exodus 3:14 (JB; NIV; NKJV).

Every name falls short of your goodness and greatness.
We can only see who you are in what is.
We ask for such perfect seeing—
As it was in the beginning, is now, and ever shall be.
Amen.

God for us is my code word for the Father. That reality is foundationally givenness. Do you understand? Reality is foundationally benevolent; it's on your side. It's not a scary universe. That's why the word *Father* is a good choice, if you've had a good father. A good father is protective of you. And again, this is attested to by the contemplative *apophatic* and the Hindi *sat*.

THE LIVING MANIFESTATION: THE CHRIST

In the second person of the Trinity, we have the visible epiphany of the Unmanifest One. First in the form of creation itself—which is "the Christ" in our shorthand—and secondly in personal form, whom we call "Jesus." Someone who reverences the first epiphany (*apophatic, sat*) is surely best prepared to rightly reverence the second—*kataphasis, chit*. Up to now, we've led many people to love Jesus, but many less were led to recognize, honor, and love the Christ. The major future task of Christian theology and practice is to finally join the two together.

My prayer understanding of Jesus is *God alongside us*, the accompanying God who walks with us, especially through the mystery of death and resurrection, of letting go and receiving. Theologians name this pattern the *Paschal Mystery*; it's the best direct and concise summary of all Jesus' teaching and experience.

The divine pattern revealed in the Trinity is loss and renewal, self-emptying and living on an expanded level, surrender and receptivity, "death and resurrection," darkness and light.

Life has no real opposite; death is merely a transitioning, which takes trust every time we walk through it.

I can probably say that Jesus is often roundly rejected as a serious model because few people want to believe in this pattern, and yet it is the big and redemptive pattern of everything. (I try to present this concept to modern and postmodern audiences in my book *Falling Upward*.)

By and large, what human beings want is resurrection without death, answers without doubt, light without darkness, the conclusion without the process.

Maybe you could say we don't like Jesus when we don't like reality. We deny *chit*, consciousness, and we escape into a flight of fantasy, banality, and unreality. Mechanical thinking takes over, and our lives run on autopilot—a spin cycle of passing pleasure and purposeless pain.

THE DYNAMISM WITHIN AND BETWEEN: HOLY SPIRIT

And finally: *God within us*, already promised by the Hebrew prophets Jeremiah and Isaiah, takes on an indwelling character. The unnamable I Am becomes writ large on our hearts, revealing the "down and in" divine characteristic present since the beginning of time. Let's call the Holy Spirit *Implanted Hope*.

When God as Holy Spirit is missing, I would put it this way: there's no inner momentum. There's no *élan vital*. There's no inner corrective, no inner aliveness that keeps people from dying from their wounds.

When the Spirit is alive in people, they *wake up* from their mechanical thinking and enter the realm of co-creative power. As in Ezekiel's vision, the water flows from ankles to knees to waist to neck as the New Earth is hydrated.[216] Like Pinocchio, we move from wooden to real. We transform from hurt people hurting other people to wounded healers healing others. Not just individually, but history itself keeps moving forward in this mighty move of Spirit unleashed.

It was said in the past that we lived in the age of the Father, and then the age of the Son; according to Joachim of Fiore in the twelfth century, we Franciscans were supposed to inaugurate the age of the Spirit. I don't think that we did, but why—from this medieval word to the latest prophecies of Great Awakenings and revival—is there this frequent hope that the age of the Spirit is impending?

---

216. See the vision in Ezekiel 47:1–12.

Perhaps what we most need is a shift in perspective, to fully enter into what's already happening. I believe it has entirely been the Age of the Spirit up till now—history doesn't stop. Creation just keeps unfolding;[217] the evolution of planets, stars, species, and human consciousness has never stopped since the very beginning, but our hierarchical, masculine-without-feminine, and thus static notion of God did not allow us to see it! We now know for certain that the universe is still expanding outward.

The Indwelling Spirit is this constant ability of humanity to keep going, to keep recovering from its wounds, to keep hoping and trying again. I think one thing we love so much about young children is their indomitable hope, curiosity, and desire to grow. They fall down, and soon they're all grins again. Another generation is going to try again to live life to the fullest. But too often, by the time they're my age they don't smile so much at all, and we ask, "What happened between six and sixty?" It has always in some form been a loss of Spirit, because if the Holy Spirit is alive within you, you will always keep smiling, despite every setback. This is the sheer joy of *ananda*.

TDD—TRINITY DEFICIT DISORDER

The third facet in our exploration of "Why the Trinity? Why Now?" is a renewed understanding of Jesus and "the Christ," as we reverse the historical effects of having essentially extracted Jesus from the Trinity in our concept of God. Let's look at some of these historical causes.

Unitarianism, a small outlying movement in Poland and Transylvania in the sixteenth century, really began to pick up steam in eighteenth-century England and America in the wake of Enlightenment rationalism. Adhering strictly to the Deism becoming fashionable at the time among educated elites, Unitarianism promised a move away from fractious and superstitious religion into seeing God as a remote First Cause, Jesus as just a fine moral teacher, and the church solely as a societal good in the world. Mostly, as their very name implies, they rejected the Trinity as outdated and incomprehensible.

On the flipside, a number of more conservative movements and denominations have surfaced over the years rejecting the Trinity, such as

---

217. See Romans 8:19–25.

Mormons, Jehovah's Witnesses, Christadelphians, Christian Scientists, and Oneness Pentecostals. The beliefs of these movements differ wildly from each other in almost all respects, but they're united in their rejection of the Trinity along the grounds of a literalistic, proof-texting approach to biblical interpretation, pointing out (as we've already covered) that the term *Trinity* doesn't appear in the pages of Scripture as such.

Well-meaning attempts by both liberals and conservatives in theology and spirituality have borne fruit worth considering, no doubt; but overall these approaches leave so many of us hungry, and we're not always quite sure why.

The Trinitarian unfolding of God's dynamic action satisfies us at a core level, and we're currently suffering from a Trinity Deficit Disorder. Here's why I think this is true…

ABSENTEE FATHER

When God-as-Father is missing or is seen largely as threatening and punitive, there is a foundational scariness and insecurity to our whole human journey—fear and competition dominates more than love. It's not a safe universe. It's not a benevolent universe. There's a terrorist god behind every rock, and I've got to protect my life because no one else will. I am not inherently participating, nor do I intrinsically belong. Life is framed in a win/lose paradigm, which we then use Jesus to resolve—in a superhuman kind of way, not a partnering kind of way. Please give this some honest thought and consideration.

If God is not *for* you, then it's all on you. Like an orphaned child, or a child with an abusive father, you grow up bereft and even bitter if there is no solid ground. You can see why so many people are so paranoid and obsessive today, and so preoccupied with weapons and security systems of every form and shape. Why their eyes tear up when they find their ancestors on Ancestry.com. When there's no underlying okay-ness to the world or to your own life, you'll believe anything and do anything to feel dignity and meaning. There's a deep alienation when you don't know the Father. There's no sense that reality is safe, personal, and strongly on your side, a sense that those of us with good human fathers took for granted.

In a fatherless society, you've got to save yourself, which a lot of Christians are attempting to do by all kinds of overcompensating "jihads" against the world and all manner of perceived threats. When there is no strong protection in your life, you have to be macho and materialistic, basically a control freak. There's no time whatsoever to smell the roses.

I believe that the immense cynicism and overwhelming fear that we see in the postmodern West could rightly be called a non-knowing of the Father. And when I say *knowing,* I'm using the term as we have in these pages—an experiential knowing. The biblical word for knowing God is often what we would call "carnal knowledge." Honestly, it's the *knowledge* of two naked bodies, intimate knowledge one for the other. This is almost shocking to poorly-trained church people. God-knowledge is not abstract knowing, which Western people prefer. Perhaps this is saying that true knowing is deeply loving! Yes!

God refuses to be known except through trustful, loving relationship. You cannot know God with your mind alone. And that's why all teachers of prayer and contemplation are teaching you to let go of your inadequate mind so you can go to that deeper, ubiquitous consciousness that we call the mind of Christ. It's really God in you knowing God, which is what real prayer journeys finally teach you.

SON: HAVE YOU SEEN ME?

Now when God as *Logos,* meaning, or logic (not *logic* in the rational sense, but logic as in the patterns of reality) is missing, there is no meaningful direction or purpose for our lives. We each have to start at zero. We have to figure it all out on our own, and how could we know how to connect the overwhelming plethora of dots? What matters and what doesn't?

The sad thing for me as a Christian is that we who are supposed to know this pattern seem, for the most part, as ignorant about it as everyone else. We do not know, believe, or trust that reality has a Paschal (*Passover*) pattern.

To put it plainly, change, death, and transformation are part of the deal!

Resurrection and renewal are the final goal and result.

The Paschal pattern is always loss and renewal. There is no renewal without loss. There is no new birth without death, and that's my critique of much of the born-again language of some evangelicals, which appears to be sharply on the wane with the Millennial generation even as it thrived among Boomers of my generation. The once-mighty movement that popularized this language loves to talk about new birth, but it doesn't talk honestly about death. They largely end up reflecting the culture wars of America instead of revealing any new or real alternative. Until there's a very real death to the old self of security, status, power, money, guns, and war, any talk of a rebirth or new self has become laughable to most of the world.

THE RELENTLESS DRIVE OF THE SPIRIT

History keeps moving forward with ever-new creativity. Admittedly, this movement is accompanied by equal and opposite push back. Look at what's happened just in the last century! For all of the horrible wars, injustice, and sin, both personal and systemic, the immense advances in consciousness, science, technology, and awareness are astounding. Most white folks didn't even know racism, sexism, or persecution of LGBTQ people was a problem in the 1960s, and in some places still don't. Today at least, many of us cannot go backward, yet this was "done unto us" by a Larger Wind. We did not do it by ourselves.

And where do these advances come from? I believe they emerge from the Holy Spirit, who never gives up on this creation and our humanity.[218] I don't think you can understand Scripture in any honest way unless you know that its primary arc is a salvation of history and creation itself, and today's individualism is regressive. All the covenants are with the people collectively—the "house" and the future. Individuals like Abraham, Noah, and David are only the instruments. The individuals are caught up in the salvific sweep of history, almost in spite of themselves, as YHWH shows mercy "to Israel and their descendants forever."[219] At this point, not to see this in the text is culpable ignorance.

---

218. See Romans 8:19–30.
219. See, for example, Genesis 13:15; Exodus 32:13.

I believe there is little consciousness of the Father in our postmodern milieu. There's not much underlying okay-ness to the felt-sense of the world right now.

There's little belief in the Son, either; little trust in the Paschal mystery.

It is the Spirit in history that seems to be driving us forward, not giving up on us—God within and in the spaces between. I've been grasping at metaphors to help us. The Spirit is like a homing device put inside of you, and all creation, too. For all of our stupidity and mistakes, there's in everything this deep, internal dignity, convinced of its own value. This divine indwelling keeps insisting, "I am what I am seeking!" This is surely what Jesus means when he says that all true prayers are already assured of their answer.[220]

It's God in you that loves God.

It's God through you that recognizes God.

It's God for you that assures you it is all finally and forever okay.

Now you're living inside the Trinitarian flow.

You are already home free!

INSIDE-OUT PRAYER

As conventionally understood, *prayer* has become a one-way attempt to influence this Other whom we call God. If we do it right, the folklore goes, this will compel God to listen to us. I always feel sorry for poor God, who is getting all these contrary messages from contrary people, all of whom are groveling and faith-ing!

Whom does God listen to? When God's getting thousands of prayers on the outcome of the Super Bowl, does another game go on in the heavenlies, with God having the angels tally up the prayers on each side to determine the outcome?

As long as we keep the power in our own pocket, the whole thing falls apart. It basically becomes silliness. But in a Trinitarian understanding of

---

220. See Matthew 7:7–8. See also 1 John 5:14–15.

reality, prayer is always entering into mutuality, a kind of relatedness in a loving, trusting way.

I don't know what to pray, or really even how.

Yet prayer is happening in me and through me. When I want to pray, I ask, "What is God desiring in me now?" If the response that arises doesn't display some of the fruits of the Holy Spirit as Paul lists them—"*love, joy, peace, patience, kindness, goodness, trustfulness* ["*faithfulness*" NIV, NKJV], *gentleness, and self-control*"—I doubt if that's the prayer of the Spirit.

But if this deep flow inside of me reveals a desire for healing, forgiveness, and reconciliation, maybe not always in the form I understand or even want, I can say with full authority, "Go with this flow and make this your prayer."

But remember: It is first of all God's prayer, and it's only secondarily yours. That's why the great Christian prayers are always prayed to the Father; all liturgy is addressed to the Father.

Why? Because we are in the Spirit. We are standing in the authority that this homing device is operating within us, and we always offer our prayers *through* the Christ.

Why did these early luminaries in the faith use this preposition, *through*? Because you are standing there in *persona Christi*, as the body of Christ with the full authority of Christ. It is not just "your" prayer. Again, that's why we don't pray *to* Christ; none of the great prayers of the liturgical churches are addressed to Christ. Have you ever noticed this? Check it out; it's shocking, really.

Why are the great written prayers all oriented this way? Why not pray to Father, Son, and Spirit?

Because this upsets the symmetry.

You *are* "Christ": You're standing there as Christ in the Spirit addressing the Father; the prayer is flowing through you. You listen for the homing device, your magnetic center. What is God desiring through me today? What is God appealing for? And all I can do is stand in that relationship and second the motion.

God, I want it, too. I desire what you desire, and I offer my prayer through Christ our Lord.

It is making yourself a part of the dance, a part of the love, a part of the communion that's already happening.

Jesus seems to teach that somehow our inclusion in the dance *matters* in the great scheme of things. This must be a furthering of the great *kenosis*—the self-emptying of God—that we really count.

Where do we get two great indications of this? In the great prayer of Mary and in the great prayer of Jesus in the garden of Gethsemane.[221]

Both of them are saying, "Let it be."

Mary, who is the personification of the human race receiving the Christ, shows us that our "let it be" matters to God—God does not come into our worlds uninvited. The Spirit needs a Mary, a body, a womb, a humanity that says, "I want you"—your yes is always God's yes.

When you want it, it will be given to you; it's that simple. *"Let it be done unto me,"* and it was done, right? This is the symbiotic nature of the Trinitarian life, of the Christian life, that we have been included as the mirror on the Rublev icon—into the table, into the dance. For some unbelievable reason, God allows us to matter and our prayers to matter; that's why it seems Jesus does teach us to offer intercessory prayers.

By all means, ask God for what you want. Jesus tells us to do this, but don't think you're spending some currency of personal worthiness to make a transaction happen. First you listen, then you speak; and this speaking, we're promised, matters in the great scheme of things.

Jesus, of course, in the garden of Gethsemane, embodies the same willingness his mother had. Not trusting his own ability to make a decision about whether to enter into his own arrest and execution, he says, in effect, "But You, Father, do it through me and in me"—this is the absolute relatedness we see in Jesus till the end.

I only do what I see the Father doing. I do nothing else except what I see him doing first, echoing his motions.[222]

---

221. See Luke 1:46–55 for Mary's prayer and Matthew 26:36–46 for Jesus' prayer.
222. See, for example, John 5:19.

Christian prayer thus becomes much more a merging than a manipulating, much more dancing than dominating, much more participation than partisanship. Those of you who want rain and those of you who want the flooding to stop both dance in the unitive center of the God who holds the rain and the dry land alike.

You rest in God, not in outcomes.

PRIMAL PRAYER

What prayer becomes, in this divine rest, is experiential knowledge of the flow. Prayer is not primarily the spoken or read word. That might be a second or third level of prayer, but not the primary one. Primal prayer is where you can in truth pray always,[223] where you can live in conscious communion with the divine indwelling, with the Spirit who was poured out so universally and graciously upon all creation, upon all nations and languages.[224] Primal prayer does not mean waiting for some mythical, projected future "spiritual" state, but waking up inside your life, right now, in the present moment.

Know that how you do anything is how you do everything! Just watch the *how* of your life—even more than the *what*—as dangerous as that sounds.

I love the way fourteenth-century Sufi mystic Hafiz put it: "I am a hole in a flute that the Christ's breath moves through—listen to this music."[225]

To be utterly given, and acting from this surrendered, creative center:

This is primal prayer.

This, to me, is holiness.

And the irony is, the very motivation for your continued search for God is gratitude for already having been given God. When you pray, it is not that you pray and sometimes God answers. When you pray, *God has already answered*. It would not have even entered your mind and heart to pray if the Wind had not just blown through you! Wow!

223. *"Pray without ceasing"* (1 Thessalonians 5:17 NKJV, KJV).
224. See Acts 2:1–13.
225. Hafiz, *The Gift: Poems by Hafiz*, trans. Daniel Ladinsky (New York: Penguin Compass, 1999), front matter, 203.

When much of early Christianity emerged, it was largely inside of a dominant Greek culture, and we basically overwrote Zeus onto the new description of God given us by Jesus. This Greek head god sat on his throne at the top of the pyramid, arbitrarily sending down thunderbolts. It was not a moral or consistent universe at all. It is no accident that the very word *Zeus* became *Deus* in Latin, or other variations of the same in other Latin- and Greek-based languages of the West.

The belief in God as Trinity had little chance of impacting ancient culture. Again, it is astounding that both John and Paul understood it so intuitively. Zeus/Deus was well ensconced in our minds. Soon, even Jesus was pictured sitting on a throne or emitting his own kind of thunderbolts; look at the Sistine Chapel.

TRANSCENDENCE DEFICIT DISORDER

Enlightened [ones] have found within themselves an essential contemplation which is above reason and without reason, and a fruitive tendency which pierces through every condition and all being, and through which they immerse themselves in a wayless abyss of fathomless beatitude, where the Trinity of the Divine Persons possess Their Nature in the essential Unity. Behold, this beatitude is so onefold and so wayless that in it every essential gazing, tendency, and creaturely distinction cease and pass away. For by this fruition, all uplifted spirits are melted and noughted in the Essence of God, Which is the superessence of all essence.[226]

How many of us can attest to having an experience even in the same universe as the beauty and majesty of God that this fourteenth-century Flemish mystic knew? We want to rush straight to the immanence of "melted and noughted," but first we need to enter by the gate of the "wayless abyss."

Or as the sometimes-prophetic Irish band U2 sings, "If you want to kiss the sky // Better learn how to kneel."[227]

---

226. John of Ruysbroeck, *The Adornment of the Spiritual Marriage*, trans. C. A. Wynschenk Dom, ed. Evelyn Underhill (Grand Rapids, MI: Christian Classics Ethereal Library), 213, http://www.ccel.org/ccel/ruysbroeck/adornment.pdf.
227. Adam Clayton, Dave Evans, Paul David Hewson, Larry Mullen, and Angelique Kidjo (U2), "Mysterious Ways," *Achtung Baby*, Universal Music Publishing Group, 1991.

What we've very understandably tried to do in modern humanistic thinking and even in the liberalism of the past several decades is to pull God down and make God chummy—things like the satirical "Buddy Christ" makeover in the "Catholicism Wow!" campaign in filmmaker Kevin Smith's iconoclastic film *Dogma*.

In reaction to the very real Zeus-like divine imagery that remains lodged in most conventional religion, we've tried to make God a little more palatable, retiring the idea of "the man upstairs" with the white beard and the endless stamina for smiting. But in rejecting the caricature, we've also denied a fuller portrait; rejecting God's transcendence altogether denies the fountainhead of God's very transformative power.

We actually end up taking away God's heart-renovating and mind-boggling ability. We can't really overcome the gap from our side; God has to do that from God's side! God's proactive actions are implicit in the dynamics of Trinity itself, and when that was incomprehensible to almost everybody, the Jesus event became God's next attempt to bridge the gap.

When we "pull" God out of the heavens, we suffer from a real transcendence deficit. Our capacity for awe is diminished, and so are we. From here, our imaginations and heart-capacities atrophy; any need to worship God disappears in boredom and malaise. Gone is any felt experience of God who is beyond, holy, and transcendent.

For the life of me, I can't see how either the smiter-with-the-mitre god or the cat-in-the-hat god can survive a serious encounter with even the visible universe! Look at the gorgeous photos coming from the Hubble telescope. As I mentioned earlier, it will take us forty thousand years before we get to the next star. Who *is* this God?

God must be utterly *beyond* in order to have any significance *within*! It's a paradox. When God is only "inside us," God becomes neutered of transforming power. I've sadly witnessed this in the cheap liberalism of the last forty years, an entire spiritual generation with no ability to kiss the ground, genuflect, or kneel; no capacity to bow, honor, or worship.

(And the same is true in too many conservative, seeker-friendly megachurches, not just the liberal mainline churches.)

"Oh yeah, I believe in God," says the pop believer, but this God is so chummy that it's not God anymore. God's been pulled inside of my tiny psyche, with no new or wonderful place to take me!

God created us in God's own image—and darn it, we've returned the favor.

INTERFAITH FRIENDSHIP

As we've touched on earlier in our exploration of *sat-chit-ananda,* Trinitarian theology is going to offer us perhaps the best foundation for interfaith dialogue and friendship we've ever had, because now we don't have Jesus as our only "trump card." This makes intelligent dialogue with other religions easier, not harder. Up to now, we've generally used Jesus in a competitive way instead of a cosmic way, and thus others hear our belief at a tribal, *"Come join us—or else"* level. A far cry from the Universal Christ of Colossians "who reconciles all things to himself, in heaven and on earth."[228] In short, we made Jesus Christ into an *exclusive* savior instead of the totally *inclusive* savior he was meant to be. As my friend Brian McLaren likes to put it, "Jesus *is* the Way—he's not standing in the way!"[229]

Once Christians learn to honor the Cosmic Christ as a larger ontological identity than the historical Jesus, then Jewish, Muslim, Hindu, Buddhist, and spiritual-but-not-religious people have no reason to be afraid of us. They can easily recognize that our take on such an Incarnation includes and honors all of creation, and themselves too.

So what's happening? It can almost be described in geometrical imagery. Maybe you sense the change happening in your soul already. Most people are raised with a monarchical, pyramidal view of reality; it starts with the parent-child relationship, but look at even the Great Seal of the United States, which is pictured on the back of every dollar bill you have ever spent. America is, of course, the rising pyramid, and when we accept God at the top of it—so the promise goes—we will be the *novus ordo seclorum,* or new world order. And *annuit coeptis* written above it asserts

---

228. See Colossians 1:20.
229. For an excellent short meditation on John 14:6—one of Jesus' most controversial statements in Scripture—see brianmclaren.net/emc/archives/McLaren%20-%20John%2014.6.pdf.

that God has "favored our undertakings" and made it all happen for us. How nice! (But is it God or Mammon that actually favors most of our undertakings?)

It is still a top-down world, and at least we are giving God the credit. But here is the crucial question: is this the credit that God wants or needs? Or is the plan much more subtle? Stay with this question! We must get back to the dance and move away from an exclusively "elevator theology."

If we understand the Trinity as the basic template of reality, our minds will slowly transition from the concept of a pyramid to a circle, which utterly changes our consciousness about...

What's really happening.

How it happens.

Where we're going.

What the goal is.

And how it is that we're a part of this eternal flow.

The important thing is the love affair.

The important thing is the dance itself.

Again, if God is Trinity, grace is intrinsic to all creatures. It's not an occasional, later additive. Grace is built into the very nature of things; indeed, its very inner dynamic is moving all things toward growth. It is the air we breathe, and it's our vocation to become who we are and all that we are. In classic theology, we call this "natural law"; everything is to live according to its true nature. But it takes awhile to know what this even is, if you have choice and will, as humans do. All plants and animals follow their natural law, although even there we find much diversity. As soon as you think it is always the female who bears the young, the seahorse appears!

So what is your true nature?

This will take you all your life to truly know, because just as God is mystery, you are the same kind of mystery to yourself. As Augustine put it in his Eucharistic liturgy for the newly baptized:

If you, therefore, are Christ's body and members, it is your own mystery that is placed on the Lord's table! It is your own mystery that you are receiving![230]

Even though I'm beyond seventy now, new relationships still astound me: I'll meet a new person, and if I can interface with them honestly, trust them, allow them, refuse to categorize or too quickly label them—it will invariably open up inside me new realms of my being that I didn't know existed until I was in relationship with them.

The late John O'Donohue puts it so exquisitely:

The Christian concept of god as Trinity is the most sublime articulation of otherness and intimacy, an eternal interflow of friendship. This perspective discloses the beautiful fulfillment of our immortal longing in the words of Jesus, who said, Behold, I call you friends. Jesus, as the son of God, is the first Other in the universe; he is the prism of all difference. He is the secret *anam cara* of every individual. In friendship with him, we enter the tender beauty and affection of the Trinity. In the embrace of this eternal friendship, we dare to be free.[231]

That's the power of relationship, and why we need to be in relationship to grow. Again, loners or separatists normally become strange and stagnant, as do people who *use* others instead of relating to them with reverence.

You are saying, in effect, *I don't need the Holy Spirit. I will find out who I am by myself, without participating in the dance. I will sit it out and just be a wallflower.*

I want to repeat, in case you've already forgotten, that there are only two things strong enough to keep you inside the dance of life:

---

230. See http://www.earlychurchtexts.com/public/augustine_sermon_272_eucharist.htm. I first saw a translation of this passage cited in Rebecca Ann Parker and Rita Nakashima Brock, *Saving Paradise: How Christianity Traded Love of This World for Crucifixion and Empire* (Boston, MA: Beacon Press, 2009), 144. This book is a fresh, breathtaking look at the first thousand years of church history from "below." See savingparadise.net.
231. John O'Donohue, *Anam Cara: A Book of Celtic Wisdom* (New York: HarperCollins, 1998), 15.

Great love and great suffering.

These open you to your deepest, truest nature. They keep you in the circle instead of climbing pyramids.

DO WE HAVE TO TALK ABOUT SIN?

Against this backdrop, sin is elegantly simple to understand: sin is whatever stops the flow. Call it hatred, call it unforgiveness, call it negativity, call it violence, call it victimhood—all the things Jesus warns us against in the Sermon on the Mount.[232] You just can't afford to do these things. They are death, always death, although God will even use these deaths in your favor, if you will allow it, leading to "negative capability."

Like a slingshot or drawn bowstring that actually creates forward momentum, *negative capability* describes those failures, that emptiness, those acts of resistance that end up being the very force and motivation that catapults us ahead. This is perhaps summed up in Paul's paradoxical observation that "the Law was given to multiply the opportunities for failing, so that where sin abounds, grace abounds even more."[233] What an amazing and courageous insight, and so totally counterintuitive! God's mercy is so infinite and resourceful that God uses even our sin for our own redemption.

In fact, is there any other pattern?

Sin is not some arbitrary list of little bad things that God tests you on; so few appear to pass this giant Entrance Exam anyway. It creates a rather dismal, depressed world. Sin is not a word for certain things that upset or hurt God. Inside the Perfect Flow, God could only be "hurt" if we are hurting ourselves, just as, in effect, the risen Jesus tenderly says to Paul, "It is hard for *you* when you push back against the goad."[234]

God is essentially saying, "It is *you* who cannot afford to be unloving; you just can't. It's going to stop the intrinsic flow, and you'll be outside the mystery; you'll be outside the flow of grace that is inherent to every

---

232. See Matthew 5–7.
233. See Romans 5:20–21.
234. See Acts 26:14.

event—yes, even sin." We are not punished *for* our sins—we are punished *by* our sins!

This is why Jesus commanded us to love. You must love. You must, or you won't know the basics. You won't know God, you won't know yourself, and you won't know the divine dance. *And some kind of suffering is always the price and proof of love.*

We all know this is many times more work than obeying the Ten Commandments. I hope you obey the Ten Commandments—I'm all for it. But it's ten times more important to live moment by moment in communion, staying in the positive flow and noting all negative resistance. This is your contemplative practice, which we originally just called *prayer.*

Flowing people heal just by being there.

Sinful people, according to how we have here described sin, tear down just by being there.

So from this more spacious place, let's again acknowledge:

God for us, we call you Father.
God alongside us, we call you Jesus.
God within us, we call you Holy Spirit.
You are the eternal mystery that enables, enfolds, and enlivens all things,
Even us and even me.

Every name falls short of your goodness and greatness.
We can only see who you are in what is.
We ask for such perfect seeing—
As it was in the beginning, is now, and ever shall be.
Amen.

ENTERING BY ANOTHER DOOR

Let me say again: God is not only stranger than we think, but stranger than the mind *can* think. Perhaps much of the weakness of our first two thousand years of reflection upon the Trinity—and many of our dogmas, for that matter—is that we've tried to enter this space through the door of our logical mind instead of through the door of prayer.

Did you know that the early meaning of "theologian" among the Desert Fathers and Mothers was *simply someone who truly prayed*, not a brilliant mental gymnast? A theologian was one who understood these inner movements, subtle energies, and interconnections. In fact, a theologian was not trusted unless he or she was, first of all, a man or woman of prayer.

Frankly, the head does dangerous and stupid things when it hijacks our nervous system. To operate out of a head disconnected from gut and heart is to court disconnection—even disaster.

But it's instinctual to our species to be connected. I think creation is endowed with a natural order accessible to us precisely because we, the observers of creation, are essentially made in the same image as the observed.

There's a principle of likeness between the observer and the observed.

All cognition is re-cognition.

You see it because it's already you.

You know it over there because you already know it in here, at the deepest level of your being. The best feedback I get from readers is, "Richard, you didn't teach me anything totally new; the words are different, but somehow in my deepest intuition I already knew what you're saying."

All a good spiritual teacher can do is give words and verbalization so that you find yourself saying, "Yes, I already know this. He may be drawing it out for me, but this insight is not coming from Richard."

If I'm not sparking recognition in you, I don't think I'm teaching in the Spirit. Because it's only the Spirit in me that knows what the Spirit in you knows, and we're both trying to hone back to that same center.

The Trinity—and its generative effect, love—is the true "theory of everything." Everybody is searching for this unifying theory lately. Triune love, it seems to me, is the resolution piece that helps us to understand, to let go, and to stand secure in the world, in the same relational way that we find God in Godself standing.

Only love, the mystics say, can finally know accurately. Now *please* don't interpret this "love" in a sentimental way, all right? This isn't saccharine, or a Hallmark special.

When the self is surrendered—when we're not too tied to our own agenda, anger, fear, or desire to make things happen our way—we are truly open to love. But be aware of the heart's propensity to clench and close.

The very act of reading books like this carries with it a certain danger. Readers approach a book with certain clear expectations. Maybe the back cover didn't say it was going to meet those expectations, but they lay implicitly in people's minds. When the content fails to conform to expectations, some readers actually feel they have a right to take offense! Do you see the narcissism in that? It doesn't show up just in reading, but also in life: I want reality to be what I want it to be.

If this is you, you're going to go through life unhappy 90 percent of the time, because the world is not going to meet your preset expectations. Every set expectation is a resentment waiting to happen.

BEING THERE

As you hold this book in your hands, see if you can fully sink into *right now—always remembering*:

You can't *get* here; there is no place to get to.

You can only *be* here.

Sisters and brothers, I believe that behind every mistaken understanding of reality, there is always a mistaken understanding of God. That might sound like too broad of a generalization, but I find it to be true. Most people don't bother to think at this theological level, nor do they need to, but if you draw close to someone who is in a violent, unhappy, or fearful state of being, you always find that their operative god (and there always is one, whether they know it or not) is inadequate, distorted, or even toxic. Everybody has their primary loyalty and reference point, even if it is merely the god of safety.

So everybody has a god, or one central reference point, whether they admit it or not. All you need is a god who is really worthy of being God. Because you will become the god you worship. Truly good people have always met a truly good God.

AN AMAZING CHAIN OF BEING

It always surprises people that there are very few sayings or stories found uniformly in all four gospels, Matthew, Mark, Luke, and John; there really aren't that many.

This is one:

Anyone who welcomes you welcomes me; and anyone who welcomes me welcomes the one who sent me.[235]

If you grew up Christian, surely you've heard that saying tossed around—maybe before the preacher asked for women to volunteer in the kitchen for fellowship hour!

But have you ever stopped to think what's really happening here? Jesus is saying there is a moral equivalence between you, your neighbor, the Christ, and God!

This is an amazing chain of being that is not evident to the casual seer. This new ontology—this new way of shaping reality—is the core and foundation of the entire Christian revelation and revolution.

This is meant to utterly reshape our understanding of *who God is* and *where God is.*

Of *who we are* and *where we are.*

Will you allow it?

God is no longer "out there," which religion, from the beginning of time, has imagined.

One must ask, "What is the new experience that allows all four Gospels to talk in such a counter-intuitive yet self-assured way?"

TRINITY IN ETERNITY PAST

But first we need to get back to the beginning—really, *before* the beginning. We need to stretch our hearts and imaginations to the pre-existent Christ, the "eternally-begotten One," spoken of in the very first chapter or

---

235. Matthew 10:40; see also Mark 9:37; Luke 10:16; John 13:20.

paragraph of John's gospel, Ephesians, Colossians, Hebrews, 1 John, and probably 2 Peter.

How did we manage to miss this? *No thing became Some thing from the very beginning!* But what was before the beginning?

This conundrum made early theologians ask, "Is the universe itself eternal?" At this point, the human mind cannot compute any more and has to give up. I plead ignorance.

Let's attempt to describe the eternal Son, remembering full well that the earliest apprentices of Jesus were—just as we are—searching for metaphors to describe this movement, this shape of God, this reality. They came up with metaphors that a lot of people don't like today, especially because we think they're masculine—which they are. But I invite you to suspend this linguistic particularity for a minute to get to its underlying meaning; then you won't be tied to the metaphor so much.

As described earlier, the Father is the mystery of total given-ness. God is given-ness itself. I hope you catch the implications of this: if God is absolute given-ness, then the flow is always and forever in one positive direction; any stumbling talk of God's anger, God's wrath, or God doing any kind of withholding is spiritually, theologically impossible.

The waterwheel only and forever flows in one direction.

Human language and biblical texts simply have to talk this way to communicate our own experiences of loss, darkness, and inner dryness.

Recall Rene Girard's idea that the Scriptures are best seen as *a text in travail*; as the biblical narrative edges forward three steps, it invariably gets scared by the implications of where the Story's going—and so it pulls back two steps. *Jesus alone is the living and dynamic Word, adjusting to the readiness capacity of every age. Written words are forever and always metaphors.* They can be nothing else. When we forget that distinction, we soon become idolatrous and eventually policemen, but seldom mystics.

Bible thumpers are invariably people who prefer the two-steps-backward portions of Scripture—they love to quote anything that's vengeful, repressive, violent, exclusionary, or fearful. *We see as we are*, and a large percentage of humanity first formed its psychic world inside the punishing, fearfully warning parent world. It is hard to change, even if it makes your life small and scared.

If you need revenge, frankly you're going to love a vengeful god. If you like war, you're going to love a warlike god, and you're going to even create a warlike god. Behind every mistaken event is a mistaken image—a mistaken understanding of God.

If you are comfortable with both the receiving and extending of friendship, you will be ready and eager for the Trinity.

You will be a witness to your own transformation. It will ask everything of you, but it will also give everything to you.

Most of us have been taught, *You should be generous and giving!*—and we often feel guilty because we're not giving enough. Fewer of us were taught how to humbly receive the same divine generosity. But when there is no flow inward, it is usually impossible to sustain the flow outward.

Let me share an astounding bit of poetry from Meister Eckhart, the wonderful fourteenth-century German Dominican mystic:

> Do you want to know
> what goes on in the core of the Trinity?
> I will tell you.
> In the core of the Trinity
> the Father laughs
> and gives birth to the Son.
> The Son laughs back at the Father
> and gives birth to the Spirit.
> The whole Trinity laughs
> and gives birth to us.[236]

God has done only one constant thing since the beginning of time: God has always, forever, and without hesitation loved "the Son," understood in this sense as *creation, the material universe, you, me*—and yes, you can equally and fittingly use "the Daughter." Remember, the quality of the relationship is the point, not gender or anything else.

---

236. Matthew Fox, trans. and ed., *Meditations with Meister Eckhart* (Rochester, VT: Bear and Company, 1983), 129.

God cannot *not* love his universally-begotten child in you, and the "part" of you that already knows and enjoys this is the indwelling Spirit.

And do you know that the flow is also in both directions? The divine child also "creates" the Father *as Father*—as any parent can attest. A parent is not truly a parent until the child returns the flow. Watch the joy or tears on a mother or father's face when their little one first says "Mama!" or "Dada!"

It's the universe in a moment.

Anything less than this laughter, liking, delighting, and loving—the world simply doesn't have time for! And neither do you.

The world is now repositioned on a totally positive ground and foundation. The bankrupt, sad storyline of guilt, shame, reward, and punishment never got Western civilization very far anyway. When you start in a hole, you never really get out of the hole. But when you start with original blessing, life only grows bigger and always much better.

THE WILDEST WAVE ALIVE

I'd like to share a portion of a favorite poem with you—"The Rose":

Near this rose, in this grove of sun-parched, wind-warped madronas,
Among the half-dead trees, I came upon the true ease of myself,
As if another man appeared out of the depths of my being,
And I stood outside myself
Beyond becoming and perishing,
A something wholly other,
As if I swayed out on the wildest wave alive,
And yet was still.
And I rejoiced in being what I was.[237]

There's so much about this poem that resonates with me, but especially the phrase "I swayed out on the wildest wave alive." I think we're all swaying on this wave, whether we know it or not. Whether it's conscious or unconscious, what has drawn you to these pages is bringing this mystery

---

237. Theodore Roethke, "The Rose," *The Collected Poems of Theodore Roethke* (New York, Anchor Books, 1974). Originally published by Doubleday and Company, 1961.

of the Trinitarian flow—the wildest wave alive—to ever-higher levels of consciousness.

It isn't enough to merely know that this wave is flowing through us; Spirit actually delights in it! The foundation of authentic Christian spirituality is not fear, but joy. Not hatred, but love. It's not terror of God but actually participation in the very mystery of God.

You see, if we're completely different than God, there is an impassable gulf between us. You can't know something that's totally different than you are; the idea of such a remote God is reflected by the Deists and Neoplatonic philosophers.

What the mystery of Trinity—this wildest wave alive—is showing us, by contrast, is that the principle of likeness is at work. The indwelling presence of the Spirit within us already knows God, already loves God, and is already in love with God. There's nothing we can add to or subtract from this! All we can do is jump on this train, which is already moving.

Most people shy away. They *are* the divine mystery, but unfortunately, they're not enjoying it. They're not drawing consciously upon their Source. If I had to give the most simple definition of a Christian, this is it: simply one who is consciously drawing upon their Source.

Not which rituals you perform. They're extraneous; they're all going to die.

Not which commandments you obey. That leaves you taking your own temperature of how worthy you are; it doesn't get you closer to God at all!

Paul made it very clear in Romans and Galatians that obeying commandments will not lead you to the experience of God. And yet I would bet 85 percent of Christians still think they're going to come to God by doing it right. There's no evidence that this works. In fact, quite the contrary. This preoccupation with being right and doing it right usually creates—forgive me for being so blunt—anal-retentive personalities. They're usually judgmental, preoccupied with themselves, and very often not in love with God, in love with life, or in love with their fellow humans.

Because you can obey commandments without being in the wildest wave alive. Ego can do that, self can do that; but God alone can bring us into this flow of Trinity.

REAL PRESENCE

You can't be present with your mind alone; the mind replays the past and frets about the future most of the time. It does not know how to be present without including the heart, the body, and the soul. Presence is a two-way and body-length mirror, and Trinity teaches us to reflect this grounded reality.

In the Catholic lineage, we taught—and I would defend—the belief in the "real presence" of Jesus in the bread and the wine in the Eucharist, or *Communion*. We were very good at maintaining that end of the spectrum, a belief in the objective presence of God in the material, physical world. Catholicism, much better than our Protestant brothers and sisters, takes Incarnation to its logical conclusions—without fully realizing it, I might add.

"If God is present in people, in history, in creation," a Catholic or Orthodox believer might wonder, "then why not also extend real presence to focus, resistance, and hopeful surrender in the lowest, humblest, and yet universal, elemental foods of bread and wine?"

If we cannot accept Presence in this piece of earth, then why should we accept it in ourselves or others? How could we? It is one and the same act of faith and leap of logic. Here Incarnation has gone full length and breadth.

But do you know what none of us did very well? We didn't teach our people how to be *present here and there and everywhere*, and unless we are present before the Presence, there is no Real Presence for us. Presence, like all true prayer—like Trinity itself—is all about "interface knowing," which I called *mirroring* earlier in the book.

That for me is the reform of all religion.

BEING AND BECOMING

Thus, if God the Father is the Un-manifest, then the Christ is the original movement into Manifestation, and you might say that the Holy Spirit is the Knower and Reminder of the universal Manifestation. The more open you are to the Holy Spirit's prompting and invitations, the wider your seeing becomes.

Now we have the basis for a very grounded eco-spirituality.

Now we have the basis for the goodness and importance of all creation, and not just the human species.

Here we have a very Franciscan spirituality of appreciation for the entire length and breadth of the great chain of being: animals and everything that's created, such as rocks, water, and plants. All manifest reality is out-flowing from this mystery, and as our mystic St. Bonaventure taught, everything is thus a footprint and a fingerprint revealing the nature of God.[238]

How different would our history, and our religious history, have been if we had known this and allowed it to be true?

If Trinity is the inner pattern of God, then Jesus—to say it one more time—is the outer, visible pattern, which contains a big surprise and frankly a disappointment for us:

Loss and renewal, loss and renewal. Death as the price of resurrection.

Remember that even our sun is dying, and it's just one minor star in a galaxy of much larger stars. It's dying to itself to the tune of six hundred million tons of hydrogen per second. The sun is constantly dying, while also giving life to our solar system and to every single thing that lives on our planet.

That's the pattern. Nothing lives long-term without dying in its present form.

Death is not the opposite of life, but the full process of life.

Life has no opposite!

That's why the early Mothers and Fathers of the Church would say a most daring thing. They would say—and this might be shocking to you reading this—that even God suffers.

Jesus is the suffering and dying of God visible for all to see.

ESSENTIAL ECSTASY

As long as we have the Zeus-notion of God that I mentioned earlier, we can't make much progress. He is a power-hungry, remote-control god at the top of the hierarchy of gods, throwing down thunderbolts and favoring

238. See Bonaventure's classic text *Journey of the Mind into God* (*Itinerarium Mentis ad Deum*).

a very few chosen ones. He is always a he; he is almighty, but not equally all-vulnerable, as our Trinity is. Our collective and cultural understanding of God, I'm sorry to report, hasn't moved much beyond the "Almighty God" language we took for granted; we haven't realized that God has forever redefined divine power in the Trinity! The Christian God's power comes through his *powerlessness* and humility. *Our God is much more properly called all-vulnerable than almighty, which we should have understood by the constant metaphor of "Lamb of God" found throughout the New Testament.* But unfortunately, for the vast majority, he is still "the man upstairs," a substantive noun more than an active verb. In my opinion, this failure is at the basis of the vast expansion of atheism, agnosticism, and practical atheism we see in the West today. "If God is almighty, then I do not like the way this almighty God is running the world," most modern people seem to be saying. They do not know that the Trinitarian revolution never took root! We still have a largely pagan image of God.

But once you experience this *changing of the gods*, you have a solid and attractive basis for *Christianity as a path*—a mystical and dynamic Christianity concerned about restorative justice and reconciliation at every level, here and now.

All you have to do today is walk outside and gaze at one leaf, long and lovingly, until you know, *really know*, that this leaf is a participation in the eternal being of God. It's enough to create ecstasy. It is not the inherent dignity of the object that matters; it is the dignity of your relationship to the object that matters—that transforms object to subject, as Martin Buber famously put it, shifting from an I-It orientation to the world to an I-Thou relationship.[239] For a true contemplative, a green tree works just as well as a golden tabernacle.

In an otherwise weak poem I once created in my journal, I wrote (wisely, I think): "All are an echoed ecstasy."

But we've been robbed! All creatures naturally allow and inherently communicate this ecstasy—except for the human species. We discriminate, decide, qualify, and dissociate almost all whom we look at instead of loving them as they are.

We're the only ones who deprive ourselves of essential ecstasy.

---

239. See Martin Buber, *I and Thou* (New York: Scribner, 1958).

If you doubt this, just watch your dog. Dogs don't stop the ecstasy. *You* get tired of them jumping up and licking you, but *they* don't. It's pure, unadulterated, fascinated *enjoyment* being a dog, apparently. And then most of them just lie down one day and die. No drama.

The dog doesn't question reality.

It doesn't anguish in existential malaise, beating its paws in the dirt and asking, *Why aren't I a duck?*

Apparently, dogs just like being dogs, mulberry trees like being mulberry trees, and bees like doing what bees do; the red snapper does not mind if we name her "red snapper," although surely she knows her real name. All things give glory to God just by being what they are.

There's only one species that resists being what it is, and that's us. Ironically, we're resisting our own happiness. This is God's suffering: that the one species whom God gave free will to has used it to say *no* to itself, and thus *no* to most other things, too. This is negative mirroring. If you refuse the ecstasy, you also bequeath the refusal.

That is probably what we mean by sin.

We largely refuse ecstasy via our mind games, our mental explanations, our theories, and our theological nit-picking.

Yes, God gave you your own remote control, just as we imagined Zeus to be operating earth by remote control. You can use yours to change to any channel you want. You can even use it to exit the whole system. I guess this is why almost all religions felt it necessary to posit the logical possibility of something like hell.[240]

Trinity proclaims that God is no remote-controller but instead lovingly operates from within. Its utter relational given-ness says that humans do have a remote control, granting us more power than we've ever imagined.

TOO GOOD TO BE TRUE?

This full participation has been just too much for the psyche to believe. That's why we've felt compelled to backtrack, creating what I think every

---

240. To explore this topic further, see Richard Rohr, "Hell, No!" (2015), CD or MP3 (www. cac.org.).

Christian church has in its own way: various flavors of debt codes, worthiness codes, test cases, ritual requirements, and achievement goals.

I want to say this as strongly as I can: If you're caught up in these numbing-out schemes, you're missing the core message of the gospel. You cannot earn something you already have. You cannot achieve something that is already freely and totally given to you.

A Trinitarian spirituality leaves guilt and shame in the dust, re-centering Christianity on—dare I say it—realization and rest. What finally motivates you in this spiritual life is *gratitude, never fear*. Even duty and obligation work well only in the short run; in the long term, they create—forgive me again—anal-retentive people. I have seen them in monasteries, in morning Masses, and in mosques all over the world.

But now you know that the waterwheel is ever turning, always forward, and animated by the river itself. Not by your pushing!

Karl Rahner, one of the architects of the Second Vatican Council and my favorite European theologian, whom I quoted previously, said it so well: "But we have to say of the God whom we profess in Christ: that he is exactly where we are, and only there is he to be found."[241]

Contemporary teacher Frank Viola puts this another way:

Within the triune God we discover mutual love, mutual fellowship, mutual dependence, mutual honor, mutual submission, mutual dwelling, and authentic community. In the Godhead there exists an eternal, complementary, and reciprocal interchange of divine life, divine love, and divine fellowship....

The church is an organic extension of the triune God....

...When a group of Christians follows their spiritual DNA, they will gather in a way that matches the DNA of the triune God—for they possess [this] same life that God Himself possesses....

...The headwaters of the church are found in the Godhead.[242]

---

241. Karl Rahner, *Foundations of Christian Faith: An Introduction to the Idea of Christianity,* trans. William V. Dych (London: Darton, Longman & Todd/New York: Seabury, 1978), 226.
242. Frank Viola, *Reimagining Church: Pursuing the Dream of Organic Christianity* (Colorado Springs, CO: David C. Cook, 2008), 35.

The mystery of community in the Trinity is the mystery of *allowing recognition*, and *inter-action*.

Think about that for about ten years!

THE INCARNATION IS THE GOSPEL

Jesus became incarnate to reveal the image of the invisible God.[243] The personal Incarnation is the logical conclusion of God's love affair with creation. Do you know why I can say this? Do you know why I can believe this? Because I see it in human beings: over a period of time, we all become what we love. God in Jesus became what God loves—everything human.

Jesus dramatically exemplified the oft-quoted line of the Latin poet Terence: "I am a human being, and nothing human is foreign to me."

And I love how Eugene Peterson puts this idea in his *Message* translation:

> *The Word became flesh and blood,*
> *and moved into the neighborhood.*
> *We saw the glory with our own eyes,*
> *the one-of-a-kind glory,*
> *like Father, like Son,*
> *Generous inside and out,*
> *true from start to finish.*[244]

Just show me what you love, and I'll show you what you're going to be like five years from now. Show me what you give time to, what your treasure is, what you give energy to—and I'll show you what you'll become.

God had to become human once the love affair began, because—strictly speaking—love implies some level of likeness or even equality. The Incarnation was an inevitable conclusion, not an accident or an anomaly. It shouldn't have been a complete surprise to us.

God was destined and determined, I believe, to become a human being, but it's still a big deal when the impossible gap is overcome from God's side

---

243. See Colossians 1:15–20.
244. John 1:14 (MSG).

and by God's choice, even if it was from the beginning. To situate it in one person in one era is the supreme example of what Walter Brueggemann calls the "scandal of particularity,"[245] which is clearly the biblical pattern. In other words, it is always a bit disappointing when YHWH seems to be teaching merely through one-time anecdotes, one people Israel, or one historical Jesus, instead of revealing universal patterns through these one-time anecdotal stories or characters. A mystic is precisely one who sees things in wholes and not just in parts; he moves the incarnate moment to read the very mind of God. Literalists get lost in the specific and find it hard to make the jump. Basically, when we talk about God, we are talking about everything. Yet when God talks to us about this "everything," he does not talk in abstractions or philosophy but through very specific stories and characters. Big truth must be presented on small stages for humans to get the point.

Maybe that's why we decorate everything in sight on December 25. This almost certainly isn't Jesus' actual birthday, but it doesn't make a bit of difference what the day is—we must deck the halls! Every table, every tree, every window, saturated with colors and light…as if to reveal its inner, hidden identity.

For a few weeks, everything must shine.

My father Francis was big into fasting, but on Christmas Day, he said, "Even the walls should eat meat!" Francis found his footing in the ecstasy of both the universal Incarnation and the scandal of the particular Incarnation; once you truly get this mystery of Incarnation, redemption is a foregone conclusion. For the Franciscans, Christmas was already Easter.[246]

You see, Incarnation, rightly appreciated, is *already* redemption—Jesus doesn't need to die on the cross to convince us that God loves us, although I surely admit that the dramatic imagery has convinced and convicted many a believer. The cross corrected our serious nearsightedness in relation to the Father, buying the human soul a good pair of glasses to clearly see the Father's love.

The Mystery of Incarnation is already revealing God's total embrace. The baby in the crib already proclaims, *I like you; I want to be one with you.*

---

245. Walter Brueggemann, *An Unsettling God: The Heart of the Hebrew Bible* (Minneapolis, MN: Fortress Press, 2009), 103.
246. See Rohr, *Eager to Love*, chapter 8, and Rohr, *Things Hidden*, chapter 9.

But you know what? It wasn't enough for our psyche. The cross did not change the mind of the Father. Father was totally given from all eternity. The cross was needed as a dramatic, earth-shaking icon to change *your* mind about God, and it still serves that purpose. I think that even movies like *The Passion of the Christ* serve the purpose to shake up the psyche, to understand there could be an *immense givenness* in creation itself.

If you believe that the Son's task is merely to solve some cosmic problem the Father has with humanity, that the Son's job is to do that, then once the problem is solved, there's apparently no need for the concrete imitation of Jesus or his history-changing teachings. Yes, we continue to thank him for solving this problem, but we've lost the basis for an ongoing communion, a constant love affair, not to mention the wariness we now have about the Father and the lack of an active need for a dynamic Holy Spirit.

The idea of God as Trinity largely fell apart once we pulled Jesus out of the One Flow and projected *our* problem onto God. *We* needed convincing, not God.

BLEEDING AND FORBEARING

When I was in India some years back, I had a profound extended meeting with a holy man. He told me many wonderful things.

This is something that stayed with me: he said a great being has two hearts—one that bleeds and one that forbears. This struck me deeply.

In the heart that bleeds, I understood that whatever you enter into union with, you will suffer with. When you choose to love, you will eventually suffer, if only at the loss of the beloved. It is as certain as the dawn. Because when you give yourself completely, the given-ness is not always— or even usually—perfectly received. It is resisted, resented, given back to you, or not even noticed.

But what is this other heart that forbears? *Forbears* is not a word that we use a lot. Indians, in my experience, sometimes use English words more precisely than Americans do, and it's a gift. Here is what he told me he meant by *forbear*: A great being stays with what she loves; she's patient, she forgives, and she allows what she loves to develop, to grow. She overlooks its mistakes, and in this sense she suffers for and with reality. This is the deepest meaning of passion; *patior* is the Latin verb meaning to suffer or to undergo reality (as opposed to controlling it).

When the holy man said that to me, I realized that he was describing Jesus: a fully great being who holds together all the contraries that we cannot hold.

Jesus forbears our brokenness so that we can do the same—for ourselves and, finally, for one another. He knows, as only the mind of God can, that what we refer to as evil is really goodness tortured by its own hunger and thirst, goodness that has not been able to experience being received and given back. "Evil" is what happens when human beings become tortured with this desire for goodness that they cannot experience. And then we do the kind of horrible things we see on our televisions and social media streams: killing each other, humiliating each other, hurting each other in abuses of power and privilege, showing a complete inability to even recognize the *imago Dei* in other beings or in ourselves.

True seeing extends your sight even further: the people you want to hate, the people who carry out the worst atrocities, are not evil at their core—they're simply tortured human beings. They still carry the divine image. Hitler and Stalin carried the divine image. Hussein and Bin Laden carried the divine image! I am not inclined to admit this, but it's the only conclusion that full seeing leads me toward. The forbearance of God toward me allows me to see the divine dance in all other broken vessels.

If I'm honest, I have to acknowledge that seeing in this way robs me of a certain privilege I've allowed myself my whole life: I have always eaten generously from the "Tree of Knowledge of Good and Evil." The categories are clear in my mind, which makes judging come naturally. Kindness and forbearance? Much less so.

As I've entered this dance more and more, God has taken away from me the power to choose who are the good folks and who are bad ones; I no longer have the freedom to choose who I show respect to, which races I feel more comfortable around, and what religions—or religious subgroups—I don't like.

"Those secular liberals!"

"Those fundamentalists!"

"Those Republican [or Democrat] idiots!"

But I've been dining my way through an alternative. Invited to a conscientious dietary shift, I eat instead from the Tree of Life, offered from the center of the archetypal Garden for all who enter the flow with bleeding and forbearing hearts. What a difference it makes: in this glorious, undifferentiated, freely-offered *life*, there is no longer a "they," there.

It's all "we."

Now *we* stand defenseless before such a Generous Outpouring, utterly vulnerable before such Infinite Mercy. The giving side from God is constant; *all* is given all the time! This Divine generosity only waits for a Mary-like womb, a beloved Son. Any bit of batter willing to receive the yeast; any bit of matter willing to receive the Feast. Any piece of dirt or stardust waiting and willing to be anointed as "the Christ."

Jesus is the one who never doubted this anointing, but we are *all* messiahs in the making as we gradually learn to receive our own anointing (Christ = the *anointed one* or *signed one* = Messiah). As a little Catholic boy, I was always told that we were all "other Christs."[247]

It is a kind of cosmic sympathy with all things, and such cosmic sympathy is the hope of the world. Any "Christ" sees Christ everywhere else; in fact, that is exactly what it means to be an anointed one.

Christ bore the mystery fully ahead of time, at the head of the Great Parade or "*triumphal procession*," as Paul calls it, so that Christ could be the first of many brothers and sisters.[248] Now we can handle it in little doses with him, in him, and through him. As I wrote earlier, these became the three great prepositions that we use to conclude the great Eucharistic Prayer:

through Christ

with Christ

in Christ

The small, isolated, or private self holds a truth this big—preparing us, in fact, to live *as Christ.*

---

247. The appellation "little Christs" was first used in semi-mockery by non-believing townspeople in Antioch within a few decades after Christ's ascension. See the account in Acts 11:19–26.

248. See 2 Corinthians 2:14 and Romans 8:29.

If you're still operating out of any kind of individualistic or small-minded spirituality, you're not going to get this. It can be experienced only through mutual presence, full-bodied attentiveness, where you can assess the flow toward you, within you, through you, and outward from what you *think* of as your self.

THE GREAT ATTRACTOR

Coventry Patmore, the nineteenth-century English poet, wrote:

This "dry doctrine" of the Trinity, or primary Act of Love, is the keynote of all living knowledge and delight. God himself becomes a concrete object and an intelligible joy when contemplated as the eternal felicity of a Lover with the Beloved, the Anti-type and very original of the Love which inspires the Poet and the thrush.[249]

You are the desiring of God. God desires all things in and through you.

And if you're feeling any desire for God growing as you read these pages, this is the Son's desire for fellowship with the Father acting itself out in and through you. This is the Holy Spirit, who is the personification of the eternal and abundant energy, life, and love between the other Two. Listen to this desiring, and wait for its deeper—its deepest—level. It will get you there, as the Holy Spirit always does.

You see, you by yourself:

You don't know how to desire God.

You don't know where to look.

You don't know what to look for.

You don't know what God's name is.

You don't know God's shape.

You originally don't know God's energy.

You will almost always look in the wrong places.

Just beautiful sunsets and not cracks in the sidewalk.

Just weddings and funerals and not the laundry room.

---

249. Derek Patmore, ed., *The Rod, the Root and the Flower* (Tacoma, Washington: Angelico Press, 2013), 111.

Look at our history. I mean, every tenth street corner, billboard, and television network is shouting "*God!*" and yet they still seem to be pretty hateful and pretty unhappy! It gives us the impression that the flow isn't necessarily happening.

Let me say this as strongly as I can: Only God in you knows God. You can just jump on board if you so desire. *That's* Trinitarian spirituality.

You and your little mind and your little self can know *about* God; you can study catechisms, all kinds of Bible verses, and systematic theologies; and you can feel real informed theologically, either on the progressive side or on the conservative side. You can walk around with a title like "Doctor of Divinity" (Catholic bishops acquire this *ipso facto* at their ordination!) or "Professor of Theology" at a famous Christian university, and still not know or love God, yourself, or your neighbor.

"To know the Lord and his ways," as the Jewish prophets put it,[250] has very little to do with intelligence and very much to do with a wonderful mixture of confidence and surrender. People who live in this way tend to be the calmest and happiest people I know. They draw their life from the inside out.

Did you know that?

I offer it to you, free for the taking.

You can be an uneducated woman cleaning hotel rooms and live in this quiet and uplifting light. I have met them often—they make eye contact, stand their ground, and smile in a genuine way.

It all comes to this: do you allow the free-flow or do you stop it by endless forms of resistance, judgment, negativity, and fear?

Just "ask, seek, and knock" as Jesus says, "*and the door will be opened to you.*"[251] Why would God offer you something you have never asked for? Or really want?

Honestly, most unhappy people I have worked with have never once asked "to know the Lord and his ways."[252] For them, prayer was just a desperate, momentary attempt to manipulate a Higher Power, forming what

250. See, for example, Hosea 6:3.
251. See Matthew 7:7–8.
252. See, for example, Psalm 25:4.

Martin Buber would call the "I-It relationship" where neither party maintains its dignity.

God cannot allow us to relate to him as if God were an "it"; nor do we let our God out of the box we created for her. We both lose our dignity.

God is completely unavailable for any manipulation or cajoling, but God is always and immediately available to the sincere seeker of love and union. God waits until you are capable of an I-Thou relationship, or edges you in that direction—just like your first failed attempt at romance once did. Only then do we have adult reciprocal relationship where both grow and become.

Then we both win, and neither party is diminished—just like the Trinity. God is a fussy Lover; God does not play hard to get, but God holds out for true partners. True love always enhances both sides, and if we're to believe many of the prophets and mystics, apparently we actually matter to God; some even said we "change" God![253] Wow! Hold on to that for now.

---

253. Since Scripture depicts God as so relational, and so frequently changing the Divine mind in response to interaction with our prayers, wishes, and actions, it is stunning that certain theological systems are in such denial about it. See this sampling of passages compiled by Greg Boyd: Exodus 32:14; 33:1–3, 14; Deuteronomy 9:13–29; 1 Kings 21:21–29; 1 Chronicles 21:15; Jeremiah 26:2–3; Ezekiel 4:9–15; Amos 7:1–6; and Jonah 3:10. For a brief summary of these passages, see reknew.org/2015/04/doesgodchangehismind.

PART III
THE HOLY SPIRIT

WHOLLY RECONCILING

The Spirit's passion is to bring her anointing of humanity in Jesus to full and personal and abiding expression in us [as unique persons], and not only in us personally, but in our relationship with the Father through the Son, and in our relationships with one another, and indeed with the earth and all creation....[254]

Until the whole cosmos is a living sacrament of the great dance of the triune God.[255]

Let's make part III a very short section of the book, shall we? That way you might remember it, or open to it haphazardly and read it.

As long as we thought of God as *a Being*, or what I am calling a noun, then this Being could clearly choose to be loving on occasion, but also not loving.

But what if the very shape of Being is first of all communion? The very nature of Being is love; or, as Teilhard de Chardin expressed, "the [very] physical structure of the universe is love."[256]

Being is an active verb, and God is an event of communion? Could it be true?

God does not *decide* to love, therefore, and God's love can never be determined by the worthiness or unworthiness of the object. But God *is Love itself.*[257] God cannot *not* love, because love is the nature of God's very being.

In Scholastic philosophy, as I mentioned earlier, we were taught that the three universal qualities of naked being ("the Transcendentals") are that being is always:

good

true

beautiful

254. Kruger, *Shack Revisited*, 247.
255. Ibid., 64.
256. Chardin, "Sketch of a Personal Universe," 72, https://cac.org/the-shape-of-the-universe-is-love-2016-02-29/.
257. See 1 John 4:8, 16.

When these three are apprehended together, we also experience the radical *oneness* of all being.

We have just described the Holy Spirit, who sustains and heals all things into Love by slowly unveiling the inherent goodness, truth, and beauty in everything.

THE DIVINE ENERGY

You can now reread the prologue to John's gospel,[258] and every time you see the term *"Word,"* or *Logos*, substitute *Relationship* or *Blueprint*, instead, and it will really help you get the message. "In the beginning was the Relationship," or "In the beginning was the Blueprint." It crescendos in when the text might be translated as "And the Blueprint took shape," or "the Relationship became visible,"[259] which is enacted when the Spirit descends on Jesus and a Voice is heard: "You are my beloved child in whom I am well pleased."[260] This exact model of relationship is then intended to be passed on to us in what Jesus calls the "baptism in the Holy Spirit."[261]

Remember, the Holy Spirit *is* the love relationship between the Father and the Son. It is this relationship itself that is gratuitously given to us! Or better, we are included inside this love. Wow. This is salvation in one wonderful snapshot.

And this same relationship shows itself in other myriad forms, such as endless animals and wildflowers, mountains and trees, every cultural attempt at art and science and medicine, all positive street theatre, and every movement for renewal. Every one of these manifestations expresses this endless desire to create new forms of life and externalized love. All things good, true, and beautiful are baptized in the one, same Spirit.[262]

The Holy Spirit shows herself as the central and healing power of absolute newness and healing in our relationship with everything else. Early-twentieth-century Anglican mystic Evelyn Underhill defined mysticism as

---

258. See John 1:1–18.
259. See John 1:14.
260. See, for example, Mark 1:11.
261. See Acts 1:4–5; see also, for example, John 1:32–33.
262. Read Ephesians 4:4–7 anew!

"the art of union with Reality";[263] the Holy Spirit is the artist painting this union through us!

Any staying in relationship, any insistence on connection, is always the work of the Spirit, who warms, softens, mends, and renews all the broken, cold places in and between things. The Holy Spirit is always "the third force" happening between any two dynamics. Invisible but powerful, willing to be anonymous, she does not care who gets the credit for the wind from nowhere, the living water that we take for granted, or the bush that always burns and is never consumed.

Within creation, you can say that God the Holy Spirit has two almost opposing tasks. First, the Spirit simply wants to be continuously multiplying, in ever-new forms of creativity and life. They say two-thirds of life forms are underneath the sea, and no human eye has ever seen one-third of them. "What is a life form without *us* to see it?" we self-centered humans might imagine. Their worth is not dependent on our knowing about them! As the psalms say in so many ways, "the heavens proclaim the glory of God."[264]

In fact, the vast majority of animals and flowers that ever existed have never been observed by a human eye. They form the universal circle of praise: simply by existing, not by doing anything right, everything offers praise to God. Everything! By being, simply being. This is the foundation. If you want to be a contemplative, that's all you need to know; everything, in being itself, is giving pure glory to God.

I have to quote the familiar poem by Gerard Manley Hopkins where he says this so perfectly:

I say more: the just man justices;
Keeps grace: that keeps all his goings graces:
Acts in God's eye what in God's eye he is—
Christ—for Christ plays in ten thousand places,
Lovely in limbs, and lovely in eyes not his
To the Father through the features of men's faces.[265]

---

263. Evelyn Underhill, *Practical Mysticism* (self-published by Renaissance Classics; printed by CreateSpace, Charleston, SC, 2012), 2.
264. See, for example, Psalm 19:1.
265. Gerard Manley Hopkins, "As Kingfishers Catch Fire," *Poems and Prose*, ed. W. H. Gardner (New York: Penguin Classics, reprinted edition, 1963), 51.

That's the mystery. It's the circle completing itself.

Now, our great and terrible gift is this: we're the only ones who can put a jam in the spokes of this circle of praise. If Gerald Manley Hopkins is my favorite poet, Annie Dillard is probably my favorite writer. Allow me to quote her, too: "We are here to witness the creation and to abet it. We are here to notice each thing so each thing gets noticed. Together we notice not only each mountain shadow and each stone on the beach but, especially, we notice the beautiful faces and complex natures of each other.... Otherwise, creation would be playing to an empty house."[266]

To withhold praise, and instead stand to the side in critique, dismissal, judgment, and categorization, sorting what is not worthy of praise—this is not the divine indwelling. This is not the image of God. This is, instead, precisely what it means to live in a state of evil or sin.

As I said, this Spirit has two jobs. First, she creates diversity, as exemplified in the metaphor of wind—just breathing out ever-new life in endlessly diverse forms.

But then the Spirit has another job: that of the Great Connector—of all those very diverse things! All this pluriform life, the Spirit keeps in harmony and "mutual deference"[267]—"so there shall be one Christ, loving Himself," as Augustine daringly put it.[268] The True Seer enjoys One Giant Ecosystem of revolving and evolving love. This seeing and this enjoying is the work of the Spirit within us. This image kindles as a burning bush that is not consumed, and is stoked as *descending tongues of fire*, creating mobile temples of people from all nations,[269] speaking a universal language of love that allows them to understand one another's diverse languages. What a great symbol on so many levels!

Fire both melts and dissolves the boundaries between relationships so we can stop hiding behind our names, our labels, our definitions and descriptions. Another word for this consuming fire is, of course, *love*. And if there has been one constant identification with the Spirit, it's precisely been the Holy Spirit as love in its implanted form—it is probably what we

---

266. David Friend and the editors of *Life* magazine, eds., *The Meaning of Life: Reflections in Words and Pictures on Why We Are Here* (Boston: Little, Brown and Co., 1991), 11.
267. See Ephesians 5:21.
268. St. Augustine, "Ten Homilies on the First Epistle of John."
269. See Acts 2.

mean by the *soul* of every single thing. Unless the whole has meaning, it is very hard to give the parts much significance. When the whole is good and connected, all the parts rise by cosmic association.

How can this fire work in our bodies? Twentieth-century, African-American philosopher, theologian, educator, and civil rights leader Howard Thurman—a mentor to Martin Luther King Jr. and many other social-change agents—writes this:

> This is a living world; life is alive, and as expressions of life we, too, are alive and sustained by the characteristic vitality of life itself. God is the source of the vitality, the life, of all living things. His energy is available to plants, to animals, and to our own bodies if the conditions are met. Life is a responsible activity. What is true for our bodies is also true for mind and spirit. At these levels God is immediately available to us if the door is opened to Him. The door is opened by yielding to Him that nerve center where we feel consent or the withholding of it most centrally. Thus, if a man makes his deliberate self-conscious intention the offering to God of his central consent and obedience, then he becomes energized by the living Spirit of the living God.[270]

As we grow in conscious awareness of this Spirit, and practice her presence in acts of giving and receiving with all creation, the fire of burning bush and descending tongues will increasingly fill all creation—not in destruction, as Jesus' apprentices once begged him to unleash on their enemies[271] in echoes of the hot-headed prophet Elijah,[272] but instead as a purifying fire that we fall into.

EVERYTHING IS HOLY NOW

Once you learn to take your place inside the circle of praise and mutual deference, all meaningful distinctions between secular and sacred, natural and supernatural, fall away. In the Divine Economy, all is useable, even our

---

270. Howard Thurman, *Disciplines of the Spirit* (Richmond, IN: Friends United Press, 1977), 21. First edition by Harper and Row, 1963.
271. See Luke 9:54.
272. See 2 Kings 1:10.

mistakes and our sin. This message shouts from the cross, and we still did not hear it!

Everything is holy now.[273] And the only resistance to that divine flow of holiness and wholeness is human refusal to see, to enjoy, and to participate.

What it comes down to is that we are each a transmitter station, a relay station. That's what we are, that's what we wonderfully are, and sadly this is somehow humiliating for the ego. I was so happy when I first preached in Germany and found out that my last name, *Rohr,* was translated as "conduit" or "pipe." Alleluia!

But my ego self is not satisfied to be a pass-through account; I want to be "Richard Rohr!" Yet this small, egoic frame of reference is going to be gone in a few years in the form that I presently identify with. All I can be is a part of the circle of praise; just knowing that I'm part of the team becomes more than enough, especially when I recognize that it was all given to me freely.

I didn't ask to be born. I thank God I was born, and I'm grateful to be here. My sister, St. Clare of Assisi, is reported to have said, as she lay dying, "Thank you for allowing me to be a human being."

There it is.

Thank God that I got my little chance to dance on this stage of life, to reflect the glory of God back to God.

Once I was able to move from pyramid thinking to circular thinking, by reason of the Trinity—ah! *Then* my mind let go of its own defenses and stopped refusing the universal dance.

T. S. Eliot described another English poet, William Blake, as a person who also lived in this dance. Eliot says of Blake:

> He understood. He was naked, and saw man naked, and from the centre of his own crystal.... There was nothing of the superior person about him. This makes him terrifying.[274]

---

273. As the song "Holy Now" (1999) attests so eloquently. See petermayer.net.
274. T. S. Eliot, *The Sacred Wood: Essays on Poetry and Criticism* (London: Forgotten Books, 2012), 140. Originally published in 1920.

Precisely because they aren't trying to push or promote themselves, a true Spirit person often occurs as "terrifying." They won't manipulate you, and you always know you can't manipulate them. Saints living in the circle dance of love are often a scary anomaly. They are not subject to our usual system of rewards, punishments, and payoffs.

They're not in it for "filthy lucre," like most of the rest of us are. Francis told us to treat money like dung! Was he naive or was he free? There is no top he needed to get to, since he had already found the top—at the bottom.

Many Spirit people strike fear in the hearts of the guardians of the status quo—or of any kind of privilege. Once you are in the "general dance," as Thomas Merton called it,[275] you have no need to make your attention-grabbing movements over in the corner.

Such people are natural myth-makers; they're natural reformers. They change reality, not even by trying to but by simply showing up in this new way with an agenda so new it's no agenda at all, beyond living as part of the circle of praise.

Their presence is contagious. Their very inner freedom calls you to match its frequency within yourself. Thus, the Spirit is mostly an energetic presence; you can often tell when a person is in the Spirit because they are simultaneously unself-conscious and radiant, connected to their own circuit. It allows them to be spontaneous and quietly original.

As Scripture attests, the Spirit blows where she will;[276] you're never going to be able to control her or categorize her. You're never going to be able to define her. You're never going to be able to put her in your conceptual or denominational pocket and say, "We've captured the Spirit, and we alone can dole her out," yet so many of us practice our religion like we're Holy Ghost-busters, building the perfect traps! The Spirit cannot be constrained through altar-call formulas, pitch-perfect theology, or any confirmation ceremony. These are often attempts to domesticate, "grieve," or "sadden" the Spirit[277] without even knowing it. It happens easily whenever

---

275. See Thomas Merton, *New Seeds of Contemplation*, reprint edition: New Directions Paperbook 1091 (New York: New Directions Books, 2007), chapter 39, "The General Dance."
276. See John 3:8.
277. See Ephesians 4:30.

we confuse the Spirit with order and control instead of energy and life. The charismatic and Pentecostal movements have much to teach the mainline churches here. For one thing, they have a much stronger record of actually healing people, emotionally, physically, and relationally.

Ken Wilber points out that much church organization is at the "mythic-membership" level of consciousness, which often breeds complacency to real human suffering, in-group smugness, and little else.[278]

I've been a priest for over forty-five years now; sometimes when I look out over the crowd at Mass, I can see a passive resistance over much of the congregation's faces. Even when I'm giving what I take to be a risky and life-giving message. They are conditioned to expect nothing. They've gotten so used to these gatherings not being meaningful that they no longer know how to allow them to touch their heart or change their mind. The Holy Spirit is again the Missing Person of the Blessed Trinity.

Without the free flow of the Holy Spirit, religion becomes a tribal sorting system, spending much time trying to define who's in and who's out—who's right and who's wrong. And surprise, we're always on the side of right!

What are the odds?

Yet refining, and any sorting that may or may not need to be done— that is the work of God. It's not our problem. It really isn't. Your problem isn't to decide who is going to heaven and who is going to hell, especially when you realize those are mostly present-tense descriptions before they are ever future destinations.

Your job is simply to exemplify heaven now. God will take it from there.

Here is the remedy when you find it hard to exemplify heaven now: *Let love happen.*

Remember, you cannot "get there"; you can only *be here.*

Love is just like prayer; it is not so much an action that we do but a reality that we already are. We don't decide to "be loving." The Father doesn't

---

278. Ken Wilber, "The Integral Vision at the Millennium" (part 1), excerpts from the introduction to volume seven of *The Collected Works of Ken Wilber* (Boston: Shambhala, 2000), www.fudomouth.net/thinktank/now_integralvision.htm.

decide to love the Son. Fatherhood is the flow from Father to Son, 100 percent. The Son does not choose now and then to release some love to the Father, or to the Spirit. Love is their full modus operandi!

The love in you—which is the Spirit in you—always somehow says yes.[279] Love is not something you do; love is someone you are. It is your True Self.[280] Love is where you came from and love is where you're going. It's not something you can buy. It's not something you can attain. It is the presence of God within you, called the Holy Spirit—or what some theologians name *uncreated grace*.

You can't manufacture this by any right conduct, dear reader. You can't make God love you one ounce more than God already loves you right now.

You can't.

You can go to church every day for the rest of your life. God isn't going to love you any more than God loves you right now. You cannot make God love you any less, either—not an ounce less. Do the most terrible thing— steal and pillage, cheat and lie—and God wouldn't love you less. You cannot change the Divine mind about you! The flow is constant, total, and 100 percent toward your life. God is for you.

We can't diminish God's love for us. What we *can* do, however, is learn how to believe it, receive it, trust it, allow it, and celebrate it, accepting Trinity's whirling invitation to join in the cosmic dance.

That's why all spirituality comes down to how you're doing life *right now.*

How you're doing right now is a microcosm of the whole of your life.

How you do anything is how you do everything.

St. Bernard says, "In those respects in which the soul is unlike God, it is also unlike itself. And in those ways in which the soul is most unlike itself, it is most unlike God."[281] Bernard has, of course, come to the same thing we're trying to say here: the pattern within the Trinity is the same as

---

279. See 2 Corinthians 1:20.
280. See Richard Rohr, *Immortal Diamond* (San Francisco: Jossey-Bass, 2013) for a thorough teaching on your True Self and how to access it.
281. Aldous Huxley, *The Perennial Philosophy* (New York: Harper Perennial Modern Classics, 2009), 11. First published by Harper & Brothers, Publishers, 1945.

the pattern in all creation. And when you return to this same pattern, the flow will be identical.

Catherine LaCugna ends her giant theological tome with this one simple sentence; it's taken her two-and-a-half inches of book to get to this one line, and its simplicity might overwhelm you, but I can't end in any better place than she does:

> The very nature of God, therefore, is to seek out the deepest possible communion and friendship with every last creature on this earth.[282]

That's the job description of God. That's what it's all about. And the only thing that can keep you out of this divine dance is fear and doubt, or any self-hatred. What would happen in your life—right now—if you accepted what God has created and even allowed?

Suddenly, this is a very safe universe.

You have nothing to be afraid of.

God is for you.

God is leaping toward you!

God is on your side, honestly more than you are on your own.

---

282. Catherine Mowry LaCugna, *God for Us: The Trinity and Christian Life* (San Francisco: HarperSanFrancisco, 1993), 411.

ACKNOWLEDGMENTS

FROM RICHARD ROHR AND MIKE MORRELL

A book is in many ways like a birth: a person (or a couple) are seen as primarily doing the beautiful, excruciating work of bringing new life into the world, but the reality is that it takes a village. So many amazing people contributed to the formation of *The Divine Dance*, and we'd like to acknowledge some of you right here. We're surely not recalling every contribution; please forgive us in advance.

At the Center for Action and Contemplation in Albuquerque, Joelle Chase, Vanessa Guerin, and Michael Poffenberger are part of our team that makes everything happen, from conferences to Daily Meditations e-mail, to in-house publications like the *ONEING Journal*, to our growing Living School. In addition to this, these three—along with Tim King, working remotely from his farm in New Hampshire—have stepped up "above and beyond" to ensure that this book is birthed not only from us, but an entire global community of engaged contemplatives and activists. Thanks to them and the entire CAC team for their work in this process.

The team at Whitaker House has been nothing but encouraging, engaged, and excited about bringing this somewhat unusual book about the Trinity into the world. From acquisitions editor Don Milam to the publishers, publicists, editors, and designers—including Bob and Christine Whitaker, Cathy Hickling, Lois Puglisi, Tom Cox, Jim Armstrong—thank you for creating a hospitable home for this project.

To Turner Simkins and Jeremy Mace at NewFire Media, and Chris LaTondresse—thank you for helping this book reach as many engaged readers as possible.

To CAC board member and literary agent Christopher Ferebee, who stewarded this book wisely.

Thanks so much to Paul Young, dear brother, for providing the inspired foreword.

Thank you to all the endorsers who see value in these words.

Naming everyone who has exerted a spiritual or literary influence on these pages would be impossible; please see the footnotes to feast on their wisdom!

FROM RICHARD ROHR

This book would never have happened if Mike Morrell had not approached me with a kind offer to take material from two of my conferences, *The Divine Dance* and *The Shape of God*, and put them into written form. Not only did he graciously and creatively send me initial sample copy, but he then did so much more by his expansion of certain ideas, arrangement of the material into sequential parts, subheadings, very creative titles, and the hard work of looking up many quotes and ideas that surely needed citation.

When he also added his own younger Generation X/Millennial-age flair, formatting, examples, and vocabulary, the result is the exciting book you now are about to read. Thank you, dear Michael. You are not a "ghost writer" but a Spirit rider!

Michael was also able to invite the inspired William Paul Young, author of the worldwide best-selling novel *The Shack*, to write the foreword, which he so kindly did—and which you can now enjoy. All three of us are now committed, along with the very kind and fully cooperative folks at Whitaker House Publishers, to reintroduce the Mystery of the Divine Trinity to a hungry world.

How presumptuous to think we could do this, but all we are really doing is riding the Flow. How can we not?

FROM MIKE MORRELL

At the risk of *mild* contradiction, this book would never have happened had Fr. Richard not taken the risk of exploring an unusual writing process with someone he knew primarily as an event organizer and publicist! Thank you, Fr. Richard, for your graciousness, trust, and enthusiasm for this project from beginning to end—especially during what has been a busy season in your life and the life of the Center for Action and Contemplation.

To my family—my wife, Jasmin, and daughters, Jubilee Grace and Nova Rain: Thank you for creating space for Hubs and Dad (respectively) to work on The Book, in addition to everything else we have going on in our rich, unpredictable life together. Your love inspires me to recognize the Love that animates the Dance!

To my "day job" that is so much more at Presence International; thank you for living what we preach, that collaboration is better than competition, and we all grow stronger together. As we continue to host "A Global Conversation for a New Earth," thank you for seeing the value in my connecting with such amazing conversation partners as Fr. Richard and the CAC.

For me, spirituality does not happen in a vacuum. Throughout all the ages and stages of my life, concrete, embodied faith communities have inspired me, challenged me, given me something to rail against, and nourished me. Here's to the spaces that have raised me, sharpened me, and taught me to dance in the light of Trinity across three decades: Douglasville First Baptist; Lithia Springs Assemblies of God; Harvester Presbyterian; the unnamed, neighborhood-based, decentralized house churches of Lithia Springs, Georgia, and Raleigh, North Carolina; the late, lamented (and aptly-named) Trinity's Place; and North Raleigh Community Church.

And finally: To you, dear reader—may these pages open your life to new stages: of communion, belonging, and living in the Flow.

APPENDIX
EXPERIENCING THE TRINITY: SEVEN PRACTICES

Let's be honest: reading about the divine dance that animates the cosmos and draws us in is nice, but to really be grounded in our daily experience, we have to put this into *practice*! How can we discover Trinity in our everyday lives and relationships?

The following exercises invite the participant into this conscious and loving flow, this movement into the Life we are calling Trinity.

They should each help you in having your own inner experience of the One Life moving in you. Unless you sincerely try them, you have no reason to say they do not "work" their mystery. The future of mature Christianity will be practice-based more than merely belief-based, which gives us nothing to argue about until we try it for ourselves.

Are you ready to open yourself—to vulnerability, to risk, to relationship? If so, let's begin!

1. *Move*: The Sign of the Cross

Going back to the first two centuries of both Eastern and Western Christianity, there emerged a simple form of body prayer, sometimes called

"Blessing Oneself" or "Signing Oneself," wherein you traced the image of the cross with your hands over the upper part of your body.

Although different movements and finger-folding evolved in different cultures, it was always accompanied by the Trinitarian formula: "In the name of the Father, Son, and Holy Spirit."

Expanding on what I wrote earlier in the book, let's look at this and see if this ancient gesture might have helpful meaning for us today, especially as we need symbols that move spiritual messages out of the head and toward a cellular and bodily knowing, what is often called "muscle memory."

First, it is very telling that one is allowed to *bless oneself*, which seems to offer the individual a certain self-confidence and spiritual authority.

Second, this self-signing also seems to be *a renaming and even a reclaiming of the self in a different identity*. In most ancient cultures and in common literary usage, when any action is preceded by the phrase "in the name of," it changes your identity into another persona, with a different authority—at least while doing that action: "I am not now speaking or acting in my personal name, but I am now standing in the identity of _____." It is not insignificant that athletes and those facing death or a difficult ordeal often sign themselves for all to see. "It's not just me here now," they are somehow proclaiming!

Third, it is often seen as both a shielding and an honoring of the body itself. We begin with the forehead, honoring our thoughts and minds as the source or the beginning point of all our decisions to act: "In the name of the Father" is certainly offering our thoughts and our mind over to God as the Ultimate Source.

Then we move directly downward, crossing over our heart, toward the solar plexus, or stomach, which is certainly blessing our own enfleshment and incarnation as the body of Christ: "And of the Son," we say.

And then, now trusting and enjoying *the flow*, we cross our body from shoulder to shoulder, again crossing the heart, and say, "And of the Holy Spirit." Note the sweep, the movement, and the fullness of both vertical and horizontal.

The whole key and sacramental power lies in your ability to do this consciously, choicefully, lovingly, and prayerfully.

This is a way for the body itself to know holy things, to honor itself as the temple and container of the Mystery, and to live with a newly-conscious and self-declared dignity.

"*Amen!*"

(To watch a video of the sign of the cross, please go to TheDivineDance. org.)

2. *Walk*: Walking Meditation

When I was young, one of my spiritual directors told me to try walking meditation when I was having trouble with exclusively sitting meditation. It turned out to be a Godsend and balance for me personally, and also allowed me to invite many other highly energetic types, "Sensate" types (on the Myers-Briggs personality profile), younger types, and macho types to literally "dip their toe" into an initial meditation practice.

That same spiritual director said that an exclusive reliance upon sitting meditation did not allow many people to expend pent-up energy; without this needed release, sitting meditation was often abandoned. At certain times in our life, we must find our core energy by consciously releasing pent-up, nervous, depressive, sexual, or even happily excited energy. Sometimes we find it by releasing it—that is walking meditation.

I have often sent groups on walking meditation exercises during retreats or done this with our students at the Living School, inviting walkers to process the experience as a group once we return. This is invariably enlightening, humorous, and truly helpful for all of us. One of our students, Jonathon Stalls, even runs a walking cooperative called Walk2Connect. com, combining many of our values spiritually, ecologically, and relationally. They encourage, invite, and train thousands of people to connect to themselves, to others, and to their surroundings by foot.

We are *made* to move this way. We simply see and listen differently when we move with others and ourselves at a walking pace and out in the real, open, and unpredictable world. Into new neighborhoods and worlds where they might otherwise never go. Walking in "pretty" places isn't often the goal, but practicing presence, connection, and reverence wherever we are, is!

My guidelines are usually simple (sometimes, I sent them out wearing our Mirror Medallion, but this will be the next practice on its own):

+ Leave alone and in silence. Return alone and in silence.

+ It is not a buddy experience; break from any need to make it chatty, pretty, or quick. *You* must do the seeing on your own and own it as your own.

+ I often noted the phrase used by Shakespeare "walking like a friar," referring to the early Franciscan custom of walking some distance behind one another as they walked from town to town—so the other person, their personality, or experience does not immediately become mine, as shoulder to shoulder walking often does. This is a good meaning to "individuation," and taking responsibility for your own thoughts, emotions, and sensations—for good and for ill. Then they can be a teacher.

+ Holy goal-lessness is your goal. The journey is the total destination.

+ Just place one foot lovingly and intentionally in front of the other, and honestly trust in *guidance*. Those who expect the Spirit, receive the Spirit.

+ Take no books or journals. "Don't think, just look" is your motto.

+ Do not come back hoping to have something profound or meaningful to say. If you do come back with something to say or write, that is fine, but profundity is not the goal. Any expectation is a disappointment waiting to happen.

+ It is what it is, and that is your teacher.

+ As Jonathan Stalls says, you are now living life at "2–3 miles an hour"— the way you are designed to. And that is very good!

+ You have a very good chance of thus experiencing the pure *flow* of the Trinity through your body.

3. Watch

(a) The Mirror Medallion

During my Lenten hermitage in 2003, I first read Catherine LaCugna's book *God with Us*. It gave me theological language for what I felt I had experienced for many days during that Lent, and I came back with an idea to help other people "live and move and have their being" inside of the same *flow.*[283]

I knew that the flow was happening at different levels—mental, spiritual, psychic—during that time, and yet when I assented to any of these, it always took shape and feeling in my body, too. This flow was always *toward me, in and through me,* and also *from me toward the outer world.* All of these seemed to be needed, or it didn't feel like an authentic Trinitarian FLOW.

So back home at the Center for Action and Contemplation, we created what we called the "mirror medallion," which we have since used at many conferences, retreats, and walking meditations, and now use with our Living School students on-site. (You may order your own—see it at the back of this book.) It doubly serves as a signal that the person wearing it wishes to keep silence at present, and to protect them from any judgments of being non-sociable. They are just being social and relational in a different way, I would hope. It serves as a very practical aid in forming "the mirror mind." And you do have to practice for a long time to create it within yourself naturally.

+ The round mirror faces outward as you wear it over your chest. It thus receives the outer world exactly as a true mirror should—without distortion, adjustment, denial, or judgment. What comes toward me first of all deserves to be honored *in its bare existence,* and then also that *it is what it is* and does not immediately need my analysis or commentary or labeling.

+ The mirror, however, also faces inward, looking directly at your soul and your heart—without judgment, symbolized by the Trinitarian "Eye of God."

+ Gazing perhaps at what you cannot or will not see: the divine image that you carry.

+ Honoring what we are often afraid to honor—our own soul.

+ The quote on the inside is from Paul: "Our unveiled gaze receives and reflects the brightness of God." There was unfortunately no room for

---

283. See Acts 17:28.

the next important part of the verse: "Until we are little by little *'turned into the image that we reflect; this is the work of the Lord who is Spirit.'*"[284]

+ It is all an invitation to allow such an "unveiling" of our face and our gaze—both from the *flow in* and also from the *flow out.*

+ And I offer one further and seldom-noted Scripture to stir this full and free *flow*. It is James 4:5. Although I have read many translations, this is my favorite: "*'The longing of the spirit* [God] *sent to dwell in us is a jealous longing.'*" Try to allow the divine flow through you as the longing, the desiring, and even the jealousy of God for your soul's response. It is a biblical theme starting in Exodus 34:14, "*Yahweh's name is the Jealous One; he is a jealous God.*"

(b) Mirroring the Divine Gaze

Invite a trusted beloved (friend, significant other, parent, or perhaps yourself through a mirror) to spend a few minutes sharing each other's gaze. Sit facing each other and begin by lighting a candle or ringing a bell. Take a couple of moments with eyes closed to find your center—the stable witness. Then open your eyes and simply look at the face of the person across from you.

Give and receive this gaze in silence, being present to the other and to the presence of Love within and without. Let your eyes, face, and body be soft and relaxed while also alert. Breathe. If your attention wanders, bring your awareness back to your partner's eyes and to the presence of Love flowing between you.

When two or three minutes have passed, ring the bell again or bring your hands together and bow to signal the close of the practice. Share a few words, an embrace, or an expression of gratitude.

4. Breath

(a) The YHWH Prayer

What was usually called the "second commandment" was often translated as "*Thou shalt not take the name of the* Lord *thy God in vain.*"[285] We Christians were told that meant we should not cuss or curse people. But

---

284. See 2 Corinthians 3:18 (JB).
285. Exodus 20:7 (KJV).

a Jewish rabbi taught me that we had it completely wrong and had missed the major point:

It was actually teaching that *any* speaking of the divine name was in vain!

Any attempt to capture the Divine Essence in any spoken word was futile; this is the best way to interpret the name that was given to Moses, usually translated as some variant of "I Am Who I Am," and in its original Hebrew form YHWH (the letters yod, he, vav, he), which we usually translate as *Yahweh.*

This was to preserve God's final unknowability, and to keep religion and believers humble about their ability to know who God is. The word was quite literally *unspeakable and unpronounceable* by any fervent Jewish believer, as it is for many to this day.

But it gets much better!

It was *also* unspeakable because it was meant to imitate and replicate the sound of human breathing in and out. Try it now!

~ First inhale. (Say *Yah* breathing inward; to do this correctly you must keep the mouth cavity completely open, not using tongue or lips.)

~ And then exhale. (Say *weh* breathing outward and again keep the channel completely open, not using the lips but letting the breath glide over your tongue.)

You cannot ever say "God" and know what you are talking about, but you *can* breathe God. In fact, this means the first word you ever "spoke" when you came out of your mother's body was the sacred Name.

Your naked existence gives glory to God by the one thing it has done constantly since birth, which is to take in and give back the breath of life—in equal portions, by the way—or you will suffocate. I think there is a lesson here!

There will be a last breath someday, and it, too, will be the sacred Name.

So right now, try setting a timer for ten minutes with no other agenda than to consciously breathe the sacred Name. And *whenever* you feel the need for greater awareness, joy, and presence in your life, stop and hear this Name in your breathing.

(b) All'h Prayer

When once teaching the YHWH Prayer to an interfaith gathering of contemplative teachers, I noticed an Islamic Sufi across from me in the circle suck in his own breath and begin to tear up as I shared with the group.

After the session ended, he quickly came over to me and asked, "Do you know the strict etymology of our Muslim name for God?"

I said that I did not, and would like to know. After all, *Allah* is also the name for God used by many Christians across the Middle East. It is simply "God" in Arabic.

He told me that *Al* is the definitive article for *The*, and if you add another *l*, it gives it special emphasis, as *The Very* or perhaps *The Only*.

He said it is most correctly spelled with an apostrophe before the *h*, although many other people spell it *Allah*, which is fine.

But then he looked straight at me, again tearing up and almost shaking. He said, "Do you know what this means? We come from the same primitive, ancient experience of God as the Jewish people, with whom we have wasted centuries in fighting and hate.

"Our name for God is *the very* 'HA!' pronounced as a strong exhalation. We have the same name for God, while imagining it is so different!"

We stood there gazing at one another in deep discovery and almost disbelief—and humble reverence before the Unspeakable One.

Feel free to try the YHWH prayer with the same breathing motion of *All'h*.

(c) The Hawaiian Prayer

While recently teaching breathing divine name prayer to a large group of Hawaiians, they grinned with excitement and broke into my teaching, unable to wait to tell me that the Hawaiian word for both "breath" and "God" is also *HA* spoken as an exhalation!

And it took till the twentieth century for us to come up with a word like the "Collective Unconscious"! The Perennial Tradition simply spoke of it as the One Spirit.

5. Seeing (in the Dark)

Lectio Divina is a way of reading Scripture and other sacred writings with the *heart*, rather than the head, driving the action. It's a way of entering into the words themselves as a means of directly experiencing the presence of God.

In the following meditations, imagine the process biblical scholar Walter Bruggemann calls *orientation, disorientation,* and *new orientation.* When we let go of painful images of God—images that no longer serve— we often feel like we're stumbling in the dark. It takes awhile for our eyes to adjust, and for us to find new footing. Baptized as we are into this Trinitarian mystery, the God of our youth once again becomes strange.

Take each of these passages and really *savor* it. Turn it over in the chambers of your heart. Take these as slowly as you'd like—one per day, even—and pay attention to any new portrait of God that emerges.

The people remained at a distance, while Moses approached the thick darkness where God was.[286]

I said to my soul, be still, and let the dark come upon you
Which shall be the darkness of God.[287]

He parted the heavens and came down;
dark clouds were under his feet.
He mounted the cherubim and flew;
he soared on the wings of the wind.

He made darkness his canopy around him—
the dark rain clouds of the sky.
Out of the brightness of his presence
bolts of lightning blazed forth.

---

286. Exodus 20:21 (NIV).
287. T. S. Eliot, "East Coker," *Four Quartets* (New York: Harcourt, Brace and Company, 1943), 14.

The Lord thundered from heaven;
the voice of the Most High resounded.[288]

Clouds and thick darkness are all around him;
righteousness and justice are the foundation of his throne.[289]

And when the priests came out of the Holy Place, a cloud filled the
house of the LORD*, so that the priests could not stand to minister*
because of the cloud, for the glory of the LORD *filled the house of the*
LORD*. Then Solomon said, "The* LORD *has said that he would dwell*
in thick darkness."[290]

I will give you the treasures of darkness
and hidden riches of secret places,
that you may know that I, the Lord,
who call you by your name,
am the God of Israel.[291]

There is in God (some say),
A deep, but dazzling darkness.[292]

Saul got up from the ground, but when he opened his eyes he could see
nothing.[293]

The darkness of faith bears fruit in the light of wisdom....

...The very obscurity of faith is an argument of its perfection.
It is darkness to our minds because it so far transcends their
weakness. The more perfect faith is, the darker it becomes. The
closer we get to God, the less is our faith diluted with the half-
light of created images and concepts. Our certainty increases with
this obscurity, yet not without anguish and even material doubt,

---

288. 2 Samuel 22:10–14 (NIV).
289. Psalm 97:2 (ESV).
290. 1 Kings 8:10–12 (ESV).
291. Isaiah 45:3 (NKJV).
292. Henry Vaughan, "The Night," http://www.bartleby.com/105/112.html. Vaughan was a
seventeenth-century Welsh poet.
293. Acts 9:8.

because we do not find it easy to subsist in a void in which our natural powers have nothing of their own to rely on. And it is in the deepest darkness that we most fully possess God on earth.[294]

Trinity, which exceeds all Being, Deity, and Goodness! You who instruct Christians in Your heavenly wisdom! Guide us to that topmost height of mystic lore which exceeds light and more than exceeds knowledge, where the simple, absolute, and unchanging mysteries of heavenly Truth lie hidden in the dazzling obscurity of the secret Silence, outshining all brilliance with the intensity of their darkness, and surcharging our blinded intellects with the utterly impalpable and invisible fairness of glories which exceed all beauty![295]

Now you say, "How shall I proceed to think of God as he is in himself?" To this I can only reply, "I do not know." With this question you bring me into the very darkness and cloud of unknowing that I want you to enter.[296]

You will…be led upwards to the Ray of the divine Darkness which exceeds all existence.[297]

Here the hyper-presence of God is experienced by the religious participant as a type of absence, for our minds are unable to make the God who is there intelligible to us.[298]

[God] *alone has endless life and lives in inaccessible light. No one has ever seen him, nor can anyone see him. Honor and eternal power belong to him! Amen.*[299]

---

294. Merton, *New Seeds of Contemplation*, 141, 134–135.
295. Dionysius the Areopagite, in *The Mystical Theology* and *The Divine Names*, trans. C. (Clarence) E. (Edwin) Rolt (Mineola, NY: Dover Publications, 2004), 191. This is an unabridged republication of *Dionysius the Areopagite on the Divine Names and the Mystical Theology* (London: Society for Promoting Christian Knowledge, and New York: Macmillan Company, 1920). Language updated for this exercise.
296. Anonymous, *The Cloud of Unknowing: and The Book of Privy Counseling*, trans. and ed. William Johnston (New York: Image Books, 1996), 46.
297. Dionysius, *Mystical Theology*, 192. Language updated for this exercise.
298. Peter Rollins, *How (Not) to Speak of God* (Brewster, MA: Paraclete Press, 2006), 87.
299. 1 Timothy 6:16 (isv).

They came to Bethsaida, and some people brought a blind man and begged Jesus to touch him. He took the blind man by the hand and led him outside the village. When he had spit on the man's eyes and put his hands on him, Jesus asked, "Do you see anything?" He looked up and said, "I see people; they look like trees walking around." Once more Jesus put his hands on the man's eyes. Then his eyes were opened, his sight was restored, and he saw everything clearly. Jesus sent him home, saying, "Don't even go into the village."[300]

6. *Praise:* A Litany Invoking the Holy Spirit

Seventy Evocative Names for God (if you let them be):

Pure Gift of God

Indwelling Presence

Promise of the Father

Life of Jesus

Pledge and Guarantee

Eternal Praise

Defense Attorney

Inner Anointing

Reminder of the Mystery

Homing Device

Knower of All Things

Stable Witness

Implanted Pacemaker

Overcomer of the Gap

Always Already Awareness

Compassionate Observer

Magnetic Center

God Compass

---

300. Mark 8:22–26 (NIV).

Inner Breath

Divine DNA

Mutual Yearning Place

Given Glory

Hidden Love of God

Choiceless Awareness

Implanted Hope

Seething Desire

Fire of Life and Love

Sacred Peacemaker

Non-Violence of God

Seal of the Incarnation

First Fruit of Everything

Planted Law

Nowhere because Everywhere

The Secret Shape of God

The One Eternal Flow

Relationship Itself

The Goodness Glue

Father and Mother of Orphans

Truth Speaker

God's Secret Plan

Great Bridge-Builder

Warmer of Hearts

Space Between Everything

Flowing Stream

Wind of Change

Descended Dove

Cloud of Unknowing

Uncreated Grace

Filled Emptiness

Through-Seer

Deepest Level of Our Longing

Attentive Heart

Sacred Wounding

Holy Healing

Softener of Our Spirit

Will of God

Great Compassion

Generosity of the Creator

Inherent Victory

The One Sadness

Our Shared Joy

God's Tears

God's Happiness

The Welcoming Within

Eternal Lasting Covenant

Contract Written on Our Hearts

Jealous Lover

Desiring of God

You who pray in us, through us, with us, for us, and in spite of us.

Amen! Alleluia!

7. Wisdom Sparks[301]

In the history of spiritual practice, both East and West, the inner work we do tends to be individually-focused. Sure, we might all be in a room together while doing so—kneeling for the liturgy as Catholics, sitting in silence as Quakers, meditating as Buddhists in the sangha—but these are essentially exercises that can also be done individually; they don't *need* another person present to be practiced!

In exploring what a truly Trinitarian spirituality looks like, we're looking to develop practices utterly reliant on "when two or more are gathered." This isn't to diminish the value or importance of solo practices, but rather to also give us a more immediate taste of the flow, vulnerability, and radical interdependence that we see showing up in the One Life of Father, Son, and Spirit.

In this spirit, I'm offering a sample "circle practice" right here—in fact, *practice* feels a bit dry considering its nature. In light of the joy and mutual giving modeled in Trinity, I prefer to call this a *game*!

You might first facilitate this exercise for a small group of friends. Then you can ask that one of them facilitate it for a group you participate in.

Round One

The Setup: Three or more participants are needed. Have everyone sit in a circle and invite them to close their eyes and consider...

The Framing: you—or the facilitator—can read aloud the sections in the shaded areas:

> So often in life, there's something we are longing to hear—from a friend, from someone in our family, or even from God.
>
> We may even find ourselves doing things that will elicit praise from others, or praying and listening intently for that still, small voice to offer wisdom, peace, and insight.

---

301. This game was developed by David Bollt and Mike Morrell as part of something they offer annually at the justice, arts, and spirituality Wild Goose Festival. It's part of an entire afternoon (or evening) of "games" they call *practicing the presence of people*. To learn more about these games, and even to potentially invite David and Mike to facilitate them in your community, go to David's website at RelationalYoga.life.

So let us take a moment to recognize that Creator God is the Originator of all—that we are living members of the body of Christ—that the Spirit sounds-through and connects all humanity—and that God's vital and communicative Being must include any community or group we may find ourselves in at any given time. Even right here, in this circle.

What if you were able to hear something you've been longing to—from the person sitting right here, beside you?

So—*is* there something you are longing to hear from someone in your life? Maybe a friend or a loved one?

If the circle needs further encouragement, ask them:

Is there a word of wisdom, acknowledgment, or encouragement that you'd like to hear from someone you care about?

Maybe this is something you have needed to hear since you were a child.

Or maybe it's something related to a current relationship or struggle.

After everyone has taken a few breaths, ask those in the circle to open their eyes. Check to see if everyone has an answer. If not, allow a few more moments for them to ponder.

Once everyone has something they realize they're longing to hear, say…

Do you have it? Good. Now I want you to *speak* what you most long to hear. But instead of us just saying it right now, I want you to turn to the person next to you and tell *them* what you've received— what you most long to hear.

Share it with your partner in just the way you'd like to hear it spoken to you.

Before you share, take a moment to connect to the spirit or intention of your words. What you're about to speak is a gift.

It's often good for whoever is leading the exercise to start first and model this intention.

Now, turn to the person next to you and share what you are longing to hear.

If you're being shared with, take a moment to let this sink in.

Then, turn to the person next to you, and share what *you* most long to hear with *them*.

Do this, with the participants going all around the circle.

Often we find that those things any one of us is longing to hear are the same as—or quite similar to—something someone else is longing to hear. It's not uncommon for there to be some uncanny coincidences that can seem to point to a higher intelligence that is at work within the group.

Examples of things that people sometimes say:

You are enough exactly as you are.

You are loved.

You are doing the best you can, and that's all that you'll ever need to do.

You are exactly where you need to be in your life right now.

Round Two:

Once again, invite participants to close their eyes and ask them to consider this new question:

Is there some advice or insight that your True Self already knows, and that would be good for you to hear right now?

If your True Self—in communion with the Helper, your Inner Observer, the Holy Spirit within you—could speak one word clearly, free from the noise and entanglements of ego, what would it be?

Call for a few silent breaths that allow time for participants to consider this word, and once again offer these "shares" around the circle, from person to person, with the instruction to connect to the sincerity and importance of the words.

Examples of things that people sometimes say:

Take more time to play; you don't have to be so serious all the time.

Enjoy the people who are in your life right now—they may not be perfect, but one day you'll realize how precious these relationships are.

Everything belongs in this journey.

You are exactly where you should be.

Round Three

For the final round, invite participants to close their eyes and consider this question:

> If there is something you imagine that God wants you to know or learn, what would that be?
>
> If there were some piece of wisdom or insight that God was inviting you to discover through your current circumstances, blessings, and challenges, what would that be?
>
> If God were to speak to you and offer you a single sentence— one that you most need to hear in your life right now—what might God say?

Allow a few breaths for participants to consider, and once again offer these shares around the circle from person to person, with the instruction to connect to the significance of the message. And be sure to instruct people to take a moment to receive what they heard before sharing with the next person.

Examples of things that people sometimes say:

I have always loved you, and I will always love you.

You are home.

You are loved.

I created you in my image; you are perfect as you are.

You are whole.

Life is an opportunity to love and be loved.

You deserve to be here.

After this last round, take some time to check with the participants to see what this was like for them. Allow some space for people to share with the group.

Explore:

> What it was like to tell these things to someone?
>
> What was it like to hear these things offered from someone else?
>
> Where there any surprises?
>
> What felt good?
>
> Was there anything that was challenging to offer or to hear?

Time and again, this exercise reveals that a profound depth of wisdom, love, and connection is available to us by simply looking to our neighbor; surely, if the universe mirrors Trinity's interconnectedness, this is what we can expect!

We may find that the still, small voice of God is being whispered to us more often than we may think, as it's offered through those around us.

Consistently, this simple experience is profoundly moving and nourishing for everyone who participates. Participants often experience feelings of joy, gratitude, and relief. Laughter and tears within the circle are common and welcome.

ABOUT THE AUTHORS

Fr. Richard Rohr is a globally recognized ecumenical teacher bearing witness to the universal awakening within Christian mysticism and the Perennial Tradition. He is a Franciscan priest of the New Mexico Province and founder of the Center for Action and Contemplation (CAC.org) in Albuquerque. His teaching is grounded in the Franciscan alternative orthodoxy—practices of contemplation and self-emptying—expressing itself in radical compassion, particularly for the socially marginalized.

Fr. Richard is the author of numerous books, including *Everything Belongs, Adam's Return, The Naked Now, Breathing Under Water, Falling Upward, Immortal Diamond,* and *Eager to Love: The Alternative Way of Francis of Assisi.* He is also Academic Dean of the Living School for Action and Contemplation. Drawing upon Christianity's place within the Perennial Tradition, the mission of the Living School is to produce compassionate and powerfully learned individuals who will work for positive change in the world based on awareness of our common union with God and all beings.

 **Mike Morrell** is the Communications Director for the Integral Theology think tank Presence International, cofounder of The Buzz Seminar, and a founding organizer of the justice, arts, and spirituality Wild Goose Festival. He is an avid writer, freelance journalist for publications including *Conspire* and *RELEVANT,* publishing consultant, author coach, and the curator of the book-reviewing community at TheSpeakeasy.info. A self-titled "opti-mystic" and leading teacher and facilitator in emerging faith spaces, Morrell explores Spirit, Culture, and Permaculture on his blog at MikeMorrell.org.

Mike also curates contemplative and community experiences via Authentic World, Relational Yoga, the ManKind Project, and (H) Opp, taking joy in holding space for the extraordinary transformation that can take place at the intersection of anticipation, imagination, and radical acceptance. Mike lives with his wife and two daughters in North Carolina.

*"Incarnation means embodiment, enfleshment.
The spiritual world is revealed in the material world.
I want to teach people to take Incarnation
to its logical conclusions."*

—Richard Rohr

LIVING SCHOOL *for*
Action *and* Contemplation

Are you ready to embody love more fully?

Embark on a two-year journey
with other seekers and core faculty
Richard Rohr, Cynthia Bourgeault, and James Finley

*"The Living School is a new synthesis of Christian learning
for which I believe the world is waiting."*

—Mark Longhurst, alumnus

Admissions are open July–September each year.
Visit cac.org/living-school to learn more.

Richard Rohr's Daily Meditations

Since 2008, the Center for Action and Contemplation has been sending Richard Rohr's email reflections to thousands of people worldwide.

The meditations consistently call readers "to do justly and to love mercy and to walk humbly with God" through contemplative prayer and action (Micah 6:8). Father Richard reframes neglected or misunderstood teachings within the Christian scriptures and tradition, revealing God's loving purpose and presence. He also integrates wisdom from other religions to help us discover our oneness and stir us to deeper love and compassion.

Father Richard's meditations are a wonderful resource for personal devotions and group study.

Sign up for free daily or weekly emails at cac.org/sign-up.

Mirror Medallion

A symbol and aid for contemplative prayer

"Our unveiled gaze receives and reflects the brightness of God until we are little by little turned into the image that we reflect. This is the work of the Lord who is Spirit."
—2 Corinthians 3:18

Richard Rohr developed this simple mirror as an inspiration for a meditation practice. Both sides of the medallion are mirrors: the blank side faces outward, receiving the outer world clearly, without distortion or judgment; the Trinitarian "Eye of God" faces the wearer, mirroring the Divine Image within.

The medallion is on a cord long enough to allow it to be worn as a necklace.

Available at store.cac.org.

(See the Appendix, pages 192–193, for Father Richard's explanation of the source and symbolism of the mirror medallion, with suggestions for meditation.)

Whoever Has Ears, Let Them Hear

Experience Richard Rohr's teaching on Trinity in a different way. This book was inspired by his original talks, *The Divine Dance: Exploring the Mystery of Trinity*. Listening to Father Richard describe the mutuality between Father, Son, and Spirit brings this dynamic relationship to life. You too are invited to sit at the table and participate in free-flowing love.

4 hours of audio available as a CD set or digital MP3 download from store.cac.org.

THE
DIVINE DANCE
Exploring the Mystery of Trinity

RICHARD ROHR, OFM

THE DANCE CONTINUES...!

The Divine Dance collaborator Mike Morrell has written a very personal bonus chapter of this book. Get it *free* by subscribing to his weekly newsletter.

Each week Mike writes about spiritual growth, culture, and creating an intentional life in deep connection with God, self, others, and our world. You can get his writing delivered free to your email inbox each week.

JOIN THE COMMUNITY AND GET YOUR *DIVINE DANCE* BONUS CHAPTER HERE: MIKEMORRELL.ORG/BONUSCHAPTER